MARK

MARK

H. A. IRONSIDE

Revised Edition

Introductory Notes by
John Phillips

LOIZEAUX
Neptune, New Jersey

First Edition, 1948
Revised Edition, 1994

MARK
© 1994 by Loizeaux Brothers

A Publication of Loizeaux Brothers, Inc.
*A Nonprofit Organization Devoted to the Lord's Work
and to the Spread of His Truth.*

Unless otherwise indicated, Scripture quotations are
taken from the King James version of the Bible.

Profile taken from *Exploring the Scriptures*
© 1965, 1970, 1989 by John Phillips.

Library of Congress Cataloging-in-Publication Data

Ironside, H. A. (Henry Allan), 1876-1951.
Mark / H. A. Ironside. — Rev. ed.
Rev. ed. of: Expository notes on the Gospel of Mark, 1948.
ISBN 0-87213-426-1
1. Bible. N. T. Mark—Criticism, interpretation, etc.
I. Ironside, H. A. (Henry Allan), 1876-1951. Expository notes on
the Gospel of Mark. II. Title.
BS2585.2.I76 1994
226.3'07—dc20   94-5184

Printed in the United States of America
10 9 8 7 6 5 4 3 2

CONTENTS

MARK
BEHOLD MY SERVANT

BY JOHN PHILLIPS

John Mark was the son of the Mary who lived in Jerusalem and whose home was one of the meeting places of the early church (Acts 12:12). John was his Jewish name and Mark was his Roman name. When Paul and Barnabas set out on their first missionary journey, John Mark went along to minister to them in the capacity of a servant (Acts 13:5). No sooner did the missionaries reach the mainland of Asia Minor, however, than Mark abandoned the enterprise and thus sowed the seeds of a later serious quarrel between Paul and Barnabas. Afterward Mark made good in the Lord's work and was even commended by Paul who had felt so strongly about Mark's desertion. It would seem that Mark was influenced strongly by Peter, and there are substantial reasons for thinking that Mark's Gospel is, in essence, the result of Peter's influence upon Mark.

It has often been pointed out that Mark's Gospel is really an expansion of Peter's sermon found in Acts 10:34-43. It begins with the ministry of John the Baptist and ends with the ascension of the Lord Jesus. In other words, Peter was Mark's chief source for his material although not his only source.

One of the world's great missionary societies has as its logo a picture of an ox. On one side of the ox is a plow; on the other side is an altar. Underneath the pictures are the words: "Ready for either!" That is exactly how Mark presents to us the Lord Jesus. In the opening chapters of the Gospel we see the plow—the Son of man giving His life in service. In the closing chapters we see the altar—the Son of man giving His life in sacrifice.

Theme of Mark

It is interesting that Mark, who at first so dismally failed as a servant, should present the Lord Jesus to us as the Servant of Jehovah, God's perfect Servant. The key verse of the Gospel is: "For even the Son of man came not be ministered unto, but to minister, and to give his life a ransom for many" (Mark 10:45). This verse gives us the clue to the analysis of the Gospel of Mark.

I. THE SERVANT GIVES HIS LIFE IN SERVICE (1–10)
  A. The Servant's Work (1–3)
   1. The Work Begun (1)
   2. The Work Belittled (2:1–3:6)
   3. The Work Blessed (3:7-19)
   4. The Work Blasphemed (3:20-25)
  B. The Servant's Words (4–5)
   1. Exact in Purpose (4:1-34)
   2. Executive in Power (4:35–5:43)
  C. The Servant's Ways (6:1–8:26)
   1. The Attitude of Others toward God's Servant (6:1-29)
   2. The Attitude of God's Servant toward Others (6:30–8:26)
  D. The Servant's Worth (8:27–9:13)
  E. The Servant's Will (9:14-29)
  F. The Servant's Wisdom (9:30–10:52)
   1. Perfect Wisdom (9:30-50)
   2. Penetrating Wisdom (10:1-31)
   3. Practical Wisdom (10:32-52)
II. THE SERVANT GIVES HIS LIFE IN SACRIFICE (11–16)
  A. He Precipitates the Crisis of Calvary (11–12)
   1. His Provoking Acts (11:1-26)
   2. His Provoking Arguments (11:27–12:44)
  B. He Portrays the Consequences of Calvary (13:1–14:31)
   1. In Public (13)
   2. In Private (14:1-31)

C. He Permits the Cross of Calvary (14:32–15:47)
   1. The Will of God (14:32-41)
   2. The Wickedness of Man (14:42–15:15)
   3. The Way of Sacrifice (15:16-47)
D. He Proves the Crime of Calvary (16)
   1. The Conquest of the Grave (16:1-14)
   2. The Conquest of the Globe (16:15-20)

God's Servant Busy

Mark's Gospel begins with God's Servant busy. His credentials are presented by John the Baptist; His companions are being taken from physical toil to be prepared for spiritual toil; and His capabilities are proven in the healing of countless sick. Satan's wilderness assault is passed over in a single verse, for the whole of Mark's Gospel shows us the Servant of Jehovah destroying the works of the devil.

God's Servant Attacked

The critics of God's Servant were soon seeking to undermine His work, for they were angered at His evident authority, His love for the lost, and His undisguised scorn for their petty religious scruples and taboos. Mark showed us the Servant as mighty in word and deed. Christ speaks with the voice that stills the storm, delivers the demoniac, heals the sick, and raises the dead. Mark presented us with a Christ who is tenderly concerned with people—with their happiness, their hunger, their hardships, their health, and even their hypocrisy. Mark told us how Jesus succored the stranger, delivered the dumb, fed the famished, rebuked the radicals, and taught those who would hearken to His words. Mark told how Peter confessed the Servant's matchless worth, and how God opened Heaven to honor Him.

God's Servant Crucified

The narrative hurries on with the Servant ever busy, pouring out His life in service that must end in sacrifice. The crisis was precipitated when Jesus rode into Jerusalem on the colt and summarily cleansed the temple. Fiercely His foes sought to trap Him in His talk, but they failed and were roundly castigated by Christ for their hypocrisy. As the last week wore on to its tragic climax, the Lord sketched an outline of the ages from the time of His rejection to the time of His triumph. In private He told His disciples what to expect in the immediate future and then led them to dark Gethsemane where, after His agony, He was betrayed by Judas and delivered over to the will of His foes. Mark described with a graphic, concise, realistic, and forceful style the sad events surrounding the trial and crucifixion of Jehovah's perfect Servant. Mark told how Jesus was buried by wealthy men and how He rose again, His work on earth being finished.

The closing verses of Mark have been much discussed and often disputed, but they seem to be in keeping with Mark's theme. They tell us of the commissioning of the disciples and of the way they went forth in the Spirit and power of the risen Lord Himself to tell the good news of the gospel.

Mark's Gospel concludes with a world vision and a task entrusted to those who love the Lord. The servants of Jehovah's Servant "went forth and preached everywhere, the Lord working with them and confirming the word with signs following." To this task all those who love Him must dedicate themselves until He comes again.

INTRODUCTION

I t is interesting to notice the differing emphases of the Holy Spirit in His presentation of our blessed Lord Jesus Christ in each of the four Gospels. In them we have four portraits of our Savior. The Gospel of Matthew sets Him forth as the King, the Messiah of Israel—hence the genealogy proving Him to be the Son of David and Son of Abraham. This also accounts for the many references to and quotations from the Old Testament Scriptures found in Matthew. The Gospel of Luke presents Him as the perfect man, the unique Son of man who came to seek and to save the lost. A singular feature of Luke's record is that of the table talk of Jesus. Is there any function better than a dinner party for allowing a man to relax and open up his heart? And in Luke we see our Lord on many such occasions. The book of Luke traces His genealogy back to Adam through Heli, the father of Mary and hence the father-in-law of Joseph (Luke 3:23). The Gospel of John tells us plainly his object was to show "that Jesus is the Christ, the Son of God; and that believing ye might have life through his name" (John 20:31). John's account shows that He is the eternal Word who became flesh for our redemption.

To Mark it fell by divine appointment to show us the Son of God acting in lowly grace and devoted subjection to the Father as the perfect servant and prophet of the holy One. Mark plunged at once into his subject. In the short space of sixteen chapters he set forth the busy Servant engaged in one work of mercy after another, hastening from place to place as He does His Father's bidding. Because we are not concerned about a servant's forebears, but rather about his ability, there is no genealogy at all in this Gospel. Instead Mark revealed Jesus' marvelous record of doing good and making known the mind of God. It has often been pointed out that Mark used a word variously translated "immediately," "straightway," "forthwith," and "anon," over forty times, and this word is found only about the same number of times in all the rest of the New Testament. "The king's business requireth haste," and Jesus was ever busy in the great work for which He came into the world.

The sacrifice of the cross is presented differently too in each Gospel. Each writer had in mind a comparison to a different Levitical offering (Leviticus 1–7). John told of the death of the Lord as the *burnt offering*—the Son laying down His life to glorify the Father in the world where He had been so dishonored by sinful men. Luke portrayed that great sacrifice as the *peace offering*—Christ making peace by the blood of His cross so that God and man may be reconciled and have hallowed fellowship together. Matthew, as becomes one whose theme is the government of God, clearly identified the work of the cross with the *trespass offering*, because of which the Lord could say, "Then I restored that which I took not away" (Psalm 69:4).

But in Mark's account we gaze in awe and wonder at the holy One made sin for us that we might become the righteousness of God in Him. The great *sin offering* is set before us—Christ dying not only for trespasses committed, but because of our sinful nature, which is made evident by our practice.

I dwell on these points because of the foolish things many have taught. For instance, some speculate that Mark's Gospel was the first effort to try to recall and set forth the story of Jesus, and that this was amplified and altered by the writers of the other Gospels, who may or may not have been the persons whose names are linked with them. But we may be assured that all such speculations are idle and vain. The imprint of the divine mind is on every page of these records, and their very differences (but never contradictions) as well as their agreements are but evidence of God's inspiration.

The Object of Mark's Gospel

Mark's supreme object was to show the Gentile world the active love of God in Jesus the Christ, who served needy men, sought after sinners, and saved all who trusted Him. If one had no other part of

Scripture but this brief Gospel, he would have enough to show any troubled heart and conscience the way of life and peace.

We need not question whether Mark may, from the human standpoint, have been indebted to Peter for much of the information conveyed. All that was written was arranged by the Spirit of God with a definite object in view.

It was given to Isaiah to prophesy of Messiah as the suffering servant of Jehovah (Isaiah 52 and 53). Moses predicted the raising up of a prophet whose word on all questions would be final (Deuteronomy 18:15-19). Mark was the evangelist chosen by the Holy Spirit to portray our Lord fulfilling these two offices of servant and prophet. But we are not to suppose that this means other aspects of His nature and character were ignored. He was never more kingly than when serving, nor more divine than when He willingly limited Himself.

Peter the Great, after he had built up the Russian empire at high cost, decided he must have a navy. But no one in Russia knew the art of shipbuilding. So Peter vacated his throne for a time, appointed his consort Catherine as regent, laid aside his royal apparel, dressed as a common laborer, and journeyed to Holland and England where he learned the art himself. He worked in the shipyards side by side with men who little dreamed of the dignity of the apparently uncouth artisan who toiled with them day by day. Peter was no less an emperor when he wrought with hammer and adz than when he returned to his throne.

Mark's Background

John Mark was the son of a wealthy woman named Mary, probably a widow, whose home was large enough to serve as a meeting place for many of the early disciples after the Pentecostal outpouring (Acts 12:12).

Mark accompanied Barnabas (to whom he was related) and Paul to Cyprus, but later returned to Jerusalem, much to the displeasure of Paul (Acts 12:25; 13:13; 15:37-39). Later, however, Mark redeemed himself and became a trusted minister of Christ and companion of Paul and Peter (2 Timothy 4:11; 1 Peter 5:13). It is like God to select the onetime unfaithful servant Mark to tell the story of the ever-faithful Servant, God's own blessed Son!

According to a well-known tradition of the early church, Mark was referring to himself when he told the story of "a certain young man" who followed Christ right up to His entry into the house of the high priest. When the guards sought to lay hold of Mark, he left the linen cloth that had enswathed his body in their hands and fled from them naked (Mark 14:51-52). The fact that no other evangelist records this incident perhaps may not be sufficient grounds for connecting it with Mark himself. On the other hand, because of its wide acceptance in early days it may possibly be the truth. In that case it would imply that young John Mark had listened to the teaching of the Lord while He was in Jerusalem. Mark's heart had gone out to Jesus so much that he thought he was ready even to die with Him, but in the hour of testing Mark fled, as did the other disciples. How many there are who really love the Lord and yet lack that moral courage that enables them to go through with Him at all costs!

As we think of this fine young man and the difficulties he faced in getting started in the service of the Lord, let us remember that later on he proved himself an efficient minister of Christ. May we be encouraged to rise above our own fears and shortcomings, counting on God to make us true ambassadors of the gospel of His Son.

As we study the record of Him who said, "I am among you as he that serveth" (Luke 22:27), may our own hearts be bowed in lowly subjection before Him. Let us yield ourselves unto the One now risen from the dead, that we may serve in the same lowly spirit that characterized Him when He was in this world. May we be content with the approval of the Father while we pass through this life comparatively unknown and unregarded.

CHAPTER ONE
THE SERVANT BEGINS HIS MINISTRY

John Prepares the Crowds (Mark 1:1-13)

Mark began his record very abruptly as he introduced the Servant of Jehovah, and then told us in a very few words of His forerunner and of His baptism and temptation. "The gospel of Jesus Christ" is God's good news concerning His blessed Son who came into this world to reveal His heart to mankind and to offer Himself as the great sin offering for our redemption.

Malachi had predicted the coming of the messenger who was to precede the Lord and prepare the people for His advent. This messenger was the voice crying in the wilderness (Isaiah 40:3) calling on Israel to prepare the way of the Lord and make His paths straight. The word rendered "Lord" in Mark 1:3 is really "Jehovah" in the Old Testament passage. So we have here a clear affirmation of the deity of our Lord Jesus Christ. He who came in such meekness and lowliness was the everlasting One who had condescended to unite His deity with our humanity, apart from its sin. He came to be our kinsman-redeemer and purchased our deliverance from sin's bondage and the judgment to which we were exposed.

John came baptizing those who confessed their sins and thus professed repentance. He baptized them in the wilderness of Judea, immersing them in the turbulent waters of the Jordan, the river that symbolized death. Multitudes went out to him from all the surrounding and contiguous territory and responded to his message. Their baptism was not in any sense a meritorious act, but it was the acknowledgment that they accepted the message and admitted their need of cleansing and forgiveness. We know from John 1:29 that these penitents were directed to the Lamb of God as the only One who could take away the sin of the world and thus make it possible for guilty sinners to become reconciled to God.

John was an Elijah-like character: a stern and serious man who dwelled in the wilderness and lived the life of an ascetic, subsisting on locusts and wild honey. He did not seek to draw attention to himself but proclaimed, "There cometh one mightier than I after me, the latchet of whose shoes I am not worthy to stoop down and unloose."

John declared that when Christ appeared He would baptize with the Holy Spirit those who received Him. This we know was fulfilled on Pentecost and afterward when the risen Christ "shed forth" the gift of the Holy Spirit, who baptized believers into one body and anointed them for service.

Next we read that Jesus came from Nazareth of Galilee and was baptized of John in the Jordan. Mark did not tell us of John's objection and how this was overcome by the Lord's explanation. We read of this in Matthew 3:13-15. The baptism of Jesus was our Lord's pledge to carry on to completion the work He had come from Heaven to perform. His pledge was ratified in Heaven, and Jesus was publicly consecrated to this service when there came a voice from above saying, "Thou art my beloved Son, in whom I am well pleased." He who had been baptized, thereby identifying Himself with confessed sinners, was declared to be the sinless One.

We have no details in Mark of the temptation, or testing, of Jehovah's Servant. We are told only that *immediately* (note the word, for it will be found often in this Gospel) the Spirit drove Him into the wilderness, that He stayed there with the wild beasts for forty days, and that He was tempted by the devil. I take it that the Holy Spirit moved Jesus to go into the wilderness in order to be tested. As man on earth He chose to be under the Spirit's direction in all things. It was fitting that He should be tested before He began His gracious ministry. His temptation was not to see if perchance He might fail and sin in the hour of stress, but rather to prove that He would not fail, because He was the absolutely sinless One. Those who impute to Jesus either a sinful nature or the possibility of sinning do Him a grievous wrong. Scripture guards against any such misconceptions when it tells us that He "was in all points tempted like as we are, yet *without sin*"—or literally, apart from sin (Hebrews 4:15, italics added). There was in Him no inward tendency to sin. The temptations were all from without and found no response whatever in His heart.

When Satan left Him, angels came and ministered to Him. He was their Creator, and they delighted to serve Him in His humiliation.

Jesus Calls His First Disciples (Mark 1:14-20)

After Herod had placed John the Baptist in confinement (in the prison of Machaerus according to early historians), Jesus, following a brief stay in Judea, went up into Galilee (John 4:3). There He began His public ministry by preaching the good news that the kingdom of God had come. Doubtlessly referring to the great time prophecy of Daniel 9, He exclaimed, "The time is fulfilled," and He called on all men to repent—that is, to judge themselves before God, and to believe the glad tidings.

"He saw Simon and Andrew . . . casting a net into the sea." These brothers had met with Jesus a short time before, but had not then been called to leave all to follow Him (John 1:39-42). Now they had reached a crisis in their lives when they must make a great decision. Observe that it was the Lord Jesus, not they, who took the initiative (John 15:16).

"Come ye after me, and I will make you . . . fishers of men." It is a mistake to attempt to apply these words to all disciples of the Lord Jesus Christ. He selected these two, and others later, in a special way for a great soulwinning ministry. But we may be assured that all who follow Him faithfully will be used of Him in some way that would not be true otherwise.

"Straightway they forsook their nets, and followed him." Their hearts had already been won for Him. Now, when the call came for fulltime public service, there was no hesitancy. It is true they had not much to leave, but for His name's sake they turned from whatever they had in the way of earthly prospects, and He made them valiant and competent workmen in the great task of winning souls to Himself.

James and John, the sons of Zebedee, were also fishermen, and John at least had known Jesus before. Possibly James had known Him also. It is evident that the Lord Jesus Christ recognized their fervency of spirit and the devotion of their hearts to Himself.

"Straightway he called them: and they left their father ... and went after him." This was a real test. They doubtless loved their father Zebedee intensely, but they put Christ and His claims first, and so forsook home and business for His sake. Think what Peter, Andrew, John, and James would have missed if they had failed to heed the command to leave all for Christ's sake. They gave up the fishing business to engage in the greatest work ever committed to man— winning souls for Christ.

The Lord called the four fishermen to become fishers of men. He saw that they were expert at and diligent in their work on the sea of Galilee, and He called and equipped them for the higher and nobler service of winning souls for Himself. We are not to conclude from this that all who follow the Lord Jesus Christ will become great soul-winners. Some are called to serve in much humbler capacities. Some have no ability to preach, or even to do effective personal work. But each one is called to serve in whatever place the Lord puts him. Some are called just to suffer for His sake. All can participate in the ministry of prayer and thereby be a real help to those who preach the Word.

Just how much time elapsed between the calling of the four fishermen-apostles and the activities recorded in the rest of Mark 1, we can only conjecture. It would seem that all occurred within a very few days.

Jesus Casts Out Demons (Mark 1:21-28)

"They went into Capernaum." Our Lord and His mother and brethren had moved from Nazareth to Capernaum, and to Jesus it was therefore home (Matthew 4:13; John 2:12). It is called "his own city" (Matthew 9:1). Here He taught frequently and performed many miracles. It was a city privileged above all others in Galilee; yet it rejected His testimony and against it He pronounced one of His most solemn woes (Matthew 11:23).

"Straightway on the sabbath day." Punctiliously Jesus observed the sabbath of the law in the way God intended that it should be kept. But He refused to recognize the mass of traditions and legalistic additions to the Scriptures that the rabbis had connected with the sabbath. The rabbis had made burdensome what was intended for blessing. The synagogue was open to Him as a recognized teacher, and He entered into it and taught.

The Synagogue in Israel. The first mention of a synagogue in Scripture is in Psalm 74:8 (KJV). The last is in Revelation 3:9, where we read of a synagogue of Satan. The word itself just means a place of gathering or assembling together. Unlike the temple, which was divinely appointed, the synagogue was a voluntary display of loyalty to the law of God. The Jews felt the need of such places where they might come together for instruction and fellowship. There was but one recognized temple at any given time, and that was in Jerusalem. There were synagogues wherever there were enough Jewish families to maintain them, and often several were in one city.

As a child Jesus was accustomed to attend the synagogue. He began early to participate in its services (Luke 4:16). Note the words, "as his custom was." He honored the place where the Word of God was read and expounded, and commanded others to honor the synagogue too, even though those who taught there were not always men of consistent lives (Matthew 23:2-3). May we not learn from Him to respect the place where God's name is recognized and His Word read, even though we may not endorse all that goes on there? We are so prone to go to extremes, either showing utter indifference to evil doctrine or unholy behavior, or taking a supercilious and self-righteous attitude toward all who do not meet our standards. It is important to realize that while we as individuals are exhorted to cease to do evil and learn to do well (Isaiah 1:16-17), we are not called to ascend the judgment seat and censure others who may be as sincere as we, but do not see everything just as we do.

"He taught them as one that had authority, and not as the scribes." These men were accustomed to repeat what their teachers had said, and did not attempt to give any authoritative instructions themselves. Jesus spoke as One sent from God. He did not need to bolster His instructions with quotations from human authorities, but preached the Word as the mouthpiece of the Father, whose representative He was. This was teaching such as the people had never heard before.

"A man with an unclean spirit." The Scriptures plainly tell us of the reality of demon possession. This was not just a Jewish superstition. On this occasion the service was interrupted by a man under the control of a wicked and unclean spirit.

"I know thee who thou art, the Holy One of God." The demon recognized the person and authority of Jesus and feared lest He was about to judge the evil spirits by confining them in the eternal prison house of the damned. Men might be incredulous regarding Christ's claims, but fallen spirits know Him for who He is.

"Jesus rebuked him." Our Lord did not desire testimony from demons. He commanded the spirit to be silent and to come out of the frenzied man. With a last vengeful effort, the demon inflicted further suffering on his poor victim, and then in unwilling obedience to the command that he was powerless to disobey, he left the man free from his awful power. The deliverance was evident to all present.

Those who filled the synagogue were thrilled when they recognized the power of Jesus over evil spirits. They questioned one another as to the meaning of it all and the source of His authority. Never before, as they had listened to the ordinary exponents of the law, had they known such a demonstration of divine approval. One told another of the remarkable thing that had taken place in the synagogue of Capernaum, until the news had penetrated all that part of Galilee. But, as after-events proved, it is one thing to recognize in Jesus a great teacher, prophet, or wonderworker, and it is quite another thing to bow in repentance before God and receive the Savior He has sent, as the Redeemer from sin.

Jesus Heals Many (Mark 1:29-34)

Originally Simon and Andrew had lived in Bethsaida. It may have been after Simon's marriage that he moved to Capernaum, possibly to share the home of his wife's mother.

"Simon's wife's mother lay sick of a fever." Everywhere Jesus went there were evidences of the havoc sin had wrought in Israel. Had this people been faithful to God, He would have taken sickness away from them (Exodus 15:26). But as a nation they had failed to obey His Word. Consequently sickness and disease were everywhere prevalent. Seeing the suffering of Simon's mother-in-law, the disciples called Jesus' attention to her, confident that He would relieve the situation.

In tender personal consideration for the poor sufferer, He took her hand and gently raised her up and "the fever left her." There was healing in His touch. His hand calmed and soothed her and brought deliverance from the fire that burned in her veins. In loving gratitude she who had lain there so helplessly, now arose and ministered to others.

As the day drew to a close, a motley crowd could be seen coming from every side, bringing the diseased and demoniacs that Jesus might administer His healing power on their behalf. "All the city was gathered together at the door." This is not mere hyperbole. Capernaum was not a large city. From every quarter its inhabitants went to the house of Simon and Andrew, impelled either by curiosity or a sense of need. Alas, the great majority of them never considered seriously their responsibility to Him who had come among them in the activity of His grace not only to heal their bodies, but also to proclaim salvation for their souls.

He healed many of their physical infirmities and delivered others from spiritual bondage to demon power, but He refused to allow the wicked spirits to declare His identity, for He would not receive testimony from the hosts of the evil one.

The sabbath on which so many were healed in Capernaum (Mark 1:21-34) may have been the sabbath immediately following the day of the miraculous draught of fishes (Luke 5:1-11). The life of our Lord on earth was one of ceaseless service. This does not imply that He was actively engaged always in teaching and healing. He found abundant time for quiet communion with the Father. Yet none of His disciples were so busily engaged as He.

The sabbath day in Capernaum is but a cross section of His entire life, which was spent in proclaiming the gospel of the kingdom and meeting the needs of men and women. The Father anointed Him with the Holy Spirit so that He might go about doing good and healing all that were oppressed of the devil (Acts 10:38) as a testimony to the divine interest in human concerns. In all this ministry He has left us an example. We waste so much time on things that do not profit. He made every moment count for the glory of God. In our lives there is so much that is of no real and lasting value. In all He said or did there was a worthwhileness that counted for eternity.

The teaching and healing ministries of the Lord Jesus Christ were ever intimately connected. The latter complemented the former, and in a sense authenticated it. His works of power proved that He was the Son of God, the Messiah of Israel and the Savior of the world. He performed no useless miracles, no merely spectacular wonders. He was not a magician seeking to astonish people by His mystic power over the elements or the minds of men. In all that He did He had in view the Father's glory and the blessing of mankind. He recognized all diseases, every physical infirmity, as primarily the work of the enemy of God and man, inasmuch as there would have been no sickness in the world if sin had not come in to mar God's fair creation. It was His prerogative to undo the work of Satan and to free sufferers from the effects of sin, both spiritually and physically. He gave to Israel a foretaste of the blessing to become universal when the kingdom of God is set up and mankind is delivered from the bondage of corruption (Romans 8:20-21).

Jesus Cleanses the Leper (Mark 1:35-45)

Following that busy sabbath in Capernaum the servant-Savior withdrew Himself a great while before sunrise into a solitary place and there spent some hours in hallowed communion with His Father. Prayer was to Him, as man in perfection, the very delight of His holy soul as He talked things over with Him who had sent Him.

As the morning advanced, Simon and others of the disciples came seeking Him. When they found Him, they told Him that there were many others desiring to see and hear Him. It was their thought evidently to recognize Him as King and endeavor to force the issue, as it were, of a break with the Roman government. But for Christ there could be no kingdom without the cross. So instead of going to greet those who sought Him, He quietly said, "Let us go into the next towns." He intimated that He had a ministry to fulfill in connection with the residents of other towns, for He had been sent to preach the gospel of the kingdom to them also. Therefore, the little party went on from town to town throughout all Galilee, and He preached in the synagogues and cast out demons.

As He was ministering in one of these places, a poor unclean leper came to Him. The leper fell down at His feet and asked to be healed of the dread disease. He was sure Jesus had power, but did not know if He was willing to use it for one so definitely under the curse of God, for such was the recognized status of a leper in Israel. He cried, "If thou wilt, thou canst make me clean." With a heart filled with compassion Jesus turned to him in grace, and not fearing possible defilement by contact with one so unclean, He put forth His hand and touched the leper. Jesus exclaimed, "I will; be thou clean." Instantly the miracle was wrought. The leprosy fled away at the command of Jesus, and the former victim of this terrible disease departed rejoicing. Jesus, who had no desire to be hailed simply as a mighty wonderworker, charged the healed man to tell no one of what had taken place. The Lord ordered the man to go first to the priest in the temple at Jerusalem, and there show himself for an examination and offer the two birds and other sacrifices that Moses had commanded, as recorded in Leviticus 14, "for a testimony unto them." One can imagine the wonder and amazement of the priest as this man presented himself for ceremonial cleansing, for such a healing was something unheard-of in Israel for centuries.

The healed man could not refrain from proclaiming abroad what he had experienced; and as a result so many crowded to see Jesus that He left the city and remained out in the country. Even there they came to Him from every quarter. It was not in human power to heal leprosy, but what no physician on earth could do Jesus had accomplished by a touch and a word! Leprosy was a constitutional disease. It worked outward from within. Because of its filthiness it is used by God as a picture of the uncleanness of sin.

Every unsaved soul is afflicted with this dread disease and is an unclean sinner in the sight of God. A man was not a leper because he had horrible ulcers and other sores on his body. These were but evidences of the disease within. And a man is not a sinner because he sins: he sins because he is a sinner, and as such he is corrupt constitutionally. Only the power of the Lord can give deliverance.

Conclusion

In the first five chapters of Mark we are called on to consider the response made by various persons to the call and testimony of the Lord during His ministry on earth. Some heard with gladness His gracious invitation to be with Him as disciples and messengers, and readily abandoned all their ordinary vocations for love of Him. Others were hesitant and fearful lest too much might be involved in subjecting themselves to His yoke. Some sought Him out because of their personal needs, whether physical or spiritual; others followed Him believing He was the promised Messiah and desiring to have a part with Him in His kingdom. But whatever the motive that led them to cleave to Him, He received them. Then He patiently instructed them, unfolding the real meaning of His mission and of that kingdom of God which it was the "Father's good pleasure to give" them (Luke 12:32). It was the Father who drew men to the Lord Jesus, and so there was a welcome for all who came (John 6:44).

The welcome of the heavenly Father is just as true today. One may come to Him because his heart is broken and he has learned that Jesus Christ heals broken hearts; another comes because of a yearning that he has sought in vain to satisfy in this poor world; another comes bowed down with shame and grief because of a wicked, wasted life; and yet another comes because he has heard that there is joy and gladness to be found in Christ. But all who come are taken up in grace and given a royal reception. All must come as sinners though, for it is only such He came to call (Matthew 9:13).

Our Lord has no stereotyped way of dealing with souls. He reveals Himself by many different means and works, according to the special needs of each individual. The great thing is that the conscience be reached and the heart drawn to Him. Whatever the reason one may have for coming to Jesus, he can be certain that he will not be turned away. The Lord values loving devotion to Himself.

CHAPTER TWO

THE WORK OF THE DIVINE SERVANT
PART ONE

Healing of the Palsied Man (Mark 2:1-12)

The Lord's early Galilean ministry was still in progress, the events of Mark 2 following closely upon those of Mark 1. Capernaum was the center from which Jesus worked out to other parts of Galilee in the early summer or late spring of A.D. 28.

The presence of Jesus in any particular place soon became known, as on this occasion when the word went out that the great healer was again in the city that He had chosen for His home. Crowds filled the house where He was staying and pressed about the door as He proclaimed the message He had come from Heaven to deliver, the word of the kingdom. This was His chief mission during His three and a half years of ministry. Healing sick bodies was secondary, though to the people it doubtless seemed to be the most important. But sickness of the soul is far more serious than physical ill-health, and to bring to men the message of life is far more important than delivering them from bodily ailments.

"One sick of the palsy, which was borne of four." Without help, this poor helpless paralytic could not make his way to Jesus, but he had four friends who were apparently firmly convinced that the Lord would give strength to the palsied limbs of the sick man. These energetic friends were determined not to fail in their endeavor to bring the afflicted sufferer directly to the wonderworking, compassionate Savior. Since they found all ordinary access to Jesus blocked by the crowd surging about the door, they carried him up onto the flat roof, generally reached by an outside stairway. There they lifted off the tiles and thatching and made a space so large that by passing cords under the pallet on which the paralytic lay, they could let the sick one down to where Jesus was teaching. One can imagine the stir and excitement of the people as the reclining man was carefully lowered to the very feet of Jesus. To Him it was no rude or unwarranted intrusion, but mute evidence of the faith of the five, who counted on Him to exercise His power on their behalf.

"When Jesus saw their faith." Faith is evidenced by works. The four friends of the helpless man showed their faith by their works. Their persistence and energy demonstrated the reality of their faith in Jesus' readiness to meet the need. Assured that their sick friend needed Jesus, they were determined that nothing would prevent his coming into the Savior's presence. Are we as much concerned about bringing our unconverted friends to Jesus as they were? It was a joy to Christ when He saw the faith of these men, for faith always glorifies God. He recognizes its presence in every honest, seeking soul and is ever quick to respond to the desire of the believing heart. He recognized the faith of the friends, and seeing that the paralytic needed something far greater than healing of the body—namely, the forgiveness of his sins—"He said unto the sick of the palsy, Son, thy sins be forgiven thee." It was a dramatic moment, and His words must have amazed the listeners, for never had they known man to speak like this.

"Certain of the scribes...reasoning in their hearts." These were legalists who knew nothing of grace and who denied the claims of Jesus to be the Son of the Father. They did not go to the Scriptures for light, but they debated among themselves what it could all mean. Filled with prejudice and determined not to believe in Jesus, they at once took issue with Him. To them it was the rankest kind of blasphemy for anyone to pretend to have authority to forgive sins. This prerogative belonged to God alone. They did not know that God revealed in flesh stood in their midst!

"Jesus perceived in his spirit that they so reasoned within themselves." They did not speak aloud, thus audibly expressing their indignation and objection to His words, but Jesus knew their thoughts (Psalm 94:11) and He answered them accordingly. "Why reason ye...in your hearts?" To be able thus to read the inmost secrets of their thought-life was another evidence of deity, for only God knows our thoughts "afar off" (Psalm 139:2).

"Whether is it easier?" So far as they were concerned, they could no more heal the sick than forgive the sinner. Jesus could do both. He chose to do the more important first.

"That ye may know that the Son of man hath power on earth to forgive sins." He would perform a miracle to reveal His authority to deliver from both sin and its effects. He therefore turned to the still helpless paralytic and commanded him to rise up and carry his bed— a pallet easily rolled together—and return healed to his home. There was power in His word. As He spoke, strength came to those limbs and the man arose, to the astonishment of all who were looking on.

The palsied man had been literally "without strength" (Romans 5:6). In his weakness he pictures all men in their sins. The word of Christ spoke strength into his paralyzed limbs, just as that same word gives new life to the one who receives it in faith.

As the people saw the paralytic rise to his feet and go away carrying his bed at the command of Jesus, they realized that divine power was active in their midst, and they gave God the glory for working so wondrously through His servant Jesus. Doubtless many wondered if He were not indeed the promised Messiah as they exclaimed, "We never saw it on this fashion." It was a new and striking exhibition of the grace and power of God.

Calling of Matthew (Mark 2:13-17)

Leaving the house where He had healed the palsied man, Jesus "went forth again by the sea side," and there taught the multitude who followed Him. He revealed to them the great truths connected with the forthcoming kingdom of God, for which Israel had waited so long.

"He saw Levi the son of Alphaeus sitting at the receipt of custom." Levi, otherwise called Matthew (Matthew 9:9-13), the author of the first Gospel, was a member of the despised publican class. He was one of the tax-gatherers in the service of Rome. They were hated because they farmed the taxes, grinding down their Jewish brothers to enrich themselves. At Capernaum there was a Roman custom-house, where all the fishermen had to bring their catches and pay a certain percent as tax. Levi was perhaps connected with this office. Evidently he had heard Jesus before and was convinced in his heart that He was the Messiah; so when the call came, he responded immediately. There was instant surrender to the claims of Christ. We see in the ready obedience of Levi, an example of what should be characteristic of all whose hearts have been won by Christ.

Christ is not only our Savior. He is also our Lord. Redemption involves much more than salvation from the guilt of and the judgment due to sin. Redemption includes our deliverance from the power and authority of Satan, the god of this world, and our glad subjection to the One who has purchased us with His own precious blood. We read, "Ye are not your own . . . ye are bought with a price" (1 Corinthians 6:19-20). Because of this, we are to acknowledge the Lord Jesus as the supreme Master of our lives. Gratitude to Him for all His grace has done would in itself demand our wholehearted recognition of His dominion over us. We are not saved by following Jesus, but because we are saved we are exhorted to follow Him.

Loyalty to Christ demands that we surrender our wills to His and seek to glorify Him in all our ways. We often hear it said that our wills must be broken, but that is poor psychology and worse theology. A broken-willed man is no longer capable of making definite decisions. Tennyson wrote, "Our wills are ours, / To make them Thine." And this is what Scripture emphasizes. We are voluntarily to yield our wills to Him who has given Himself for us, that our service may be the glad, happy obedience of those who delight in the will of God above all else. We need to beware of calling Jesus "Lord" if we are slighting His commands. It is by obedience that we prove our love for Him (John 14:15), as did Levi.

As he began his new career, Levi made a feast to which he invited many of his former friends and Jesus and His disciples. It was his way of testifying to the new allegiance, and this testimony must have made a great impression on his old associates.

"The scribes and Pharisees saw him [Jesus] eat with publicans and sinners." In the eyes of these religious formalists this was a very serious offense. But it showed how little they understood the nature of the mission of Jesus. As a physician ministers to the sick rather than to the well, so Christ came to bring the message of grace to needy sinners rather than to seek out those who fancied they were already good enough for God. Actually, "there is none righteous" (Romans 3:10), but there are many who pride themselves on a righteousness they do not really possess. For such there is no blessing. It is the confessed sinner who finds mercy.

Defending His Disciples (Mark 2:18-22)

A question arose concerning fasting. Jesus took occasion to open up important truth in this connection. It was the disciples of John and those of the Pharisees, the orthodox party in Judaism, who raised the question as to why the disciples of Jesus did not follow their example in regard to fasting. Both groups evidently thought of refraining from food at certain times as meritorious, or at least advantageous in producing holiness of heart and life. It seemed therefore to them that Christ's disciples, in this respect at least, moved on a lower plane than they. Jesus answered them by putting a question: "Can the children of the bridechamber fast, while the bridegroom is with them? as long as they have the bridegroom with them, they cannot fast." Jesus was saying that there was no occasion for His followers to mourn before God and to afflict their souls while He Himself, the source of all blessing, was with them. But Jesus foretold the time when He, the bridegroom, would be taken away from them, and then they would fast in a very real sense. Their fasting would be characterized by abstinence from the follies of the world—that world which was to be arrayed against them in bitter opposition to the teachings of their Master.

Moreover, those who raised the question about fasting did not realize that Jesus had come to introduce an altogether new order. We are told elsewhere that the law was given by Moses—and there was much in the law that had to do with fasting—but grace and truth came by Jesus Christ. It was not in accordance with His program to call men and women to subject themselves to legal principles. To do so would be but to attempt to sew a piece of new cloth on an old garment, which would only result in making the tear worse. Or it would be like putting new wine into old skin bottles; when the wine began to ferment, the bottles would burst and the wine would be lost. It is not possible to put the new wine of grace into the forms and enactments of the law; the one necessarily nullifies the other. As we read in Romans 11:6, "And if by grace, then is it no more of works: otherwise grace is no more grace. But if it be of works, then is it no more grace: otherwise work is no more work." By His answer our Lord clearly distinguished between the legality of the past and the grace He had come to reveal. This was in measure illustrated in the incident related next.

Answering Questions on Sabbath Day Observance (Mark 2:23-28)

As the disciples walked through a grainfield on the sabbath day they began to pluck some of the heads of grain, rub them in their hands, and eat the grains. This was in full accord with the provision made in the law, for God had said through Moses, "When thou comest into the standing corn of thy neighbour, then thou mayest pluck the ears with thine hand; but thou shalt not move a sickle unto thy neighbour's standing corn" (Deuteronomy 23:25). But the Pharisees immediately found fault because the disciples were plucking the grain on the sabbath day, and so those legalists immediately objected.

There was nothing in the law that declared this act contrary to anything that God had commanded, but the Pharisees had added so many traditions to the law that the disciples seemed to be violating a divine precept. In reply Jesus referred to what David did when he and his men were hungry and came to the tabernacle in the days of the high priest Abiathar. David asked for food for himself and his retainers. The priest Ahimelech, the father of Abiathar, replied that they had no bread at hand except the shewbread that had been taken from the holy table and was the food of the priests (Leviticus 24:9; 1 Samuel 21:6). At David's request, however, the shewbread was given to the hungry men, and no judgment followed. When God's anointed was rejected, it was far more important to minister to him and to the needs of his followers than to preserve punctiliously the order of the tabernacle, for after all, men are more important to God than ordinances.

After referring to David Jesus declared, "The sabbath was made for man, and not man for the sabbath: Therefore the Son of man is Lord also of the sabbath." With these words He was announcing His own deity, for again and again the sabbath is called "the sabbath of Jehovah." When Jesus declared Himself to be Lord of that day of rest, He definitely confessed Himself to be the God of Israel, revealed in flesh. If the Pharisees had ears to hear, they would have understood.

I do not here go into the critical question as to the expression, "in the days of Abiathar." This has been discussed by many, and perhaps it will never be fully explained until we know even as we are known. We should remember that it would be a simple matter for some copyist to substitute by mistake "Abiathar" for "Ahimelech." On the other hand, there may be some divine reason for setting the father to one side and recognizing the son as the rightful high priest at that time.

Conclusion

We have noticed already that our Lord performed miracles in order to relieve human misery and to authenticate His messiahship. We would also emphasize the precious truth that these miracles were intended to reveal to men: the grace and tender compassion of God. Through Christ God demonstrated His deep concern for those who had brought such dire trouble and affliction on themselves by turning away from Him. The entire human race was suffering because of sin. Israel in particular had been promised immunity from disease if obedient to the law of God (Exodus 23:25). Every blind, deaf, crippled, or diseased person among them was a witness to Israel's failure in this respect (Deuteronomy 28:15ff.). In healing the sick, Jesus was undoing the work of the devil (Acts 10:38) and fulfilling what had been predicted concerning the Servant of Jehovah, Israel's promised Messiah-King (Isaiah 35:4-6). When Jesus was on earth proclaiming the gospel of the kingdom, it was specially fitting that the blessings of the coming age should be revealed. Through Christ's ministry the people were given a sample of what Israel and the whole world will enjoy in its fullness when God's King reigns on mount Zion and blessing goes out to all the earth.

Physical healing and forgiveness of sins were intimately connected in the Old Testament (Psalm 103:3; 67:2; Isaiah 58:8). This
connection between healing and forgiveness was equally true in our
Lord's earthly ministry, as Mark 2:1-12 makes clear. John prayed for
Gaius that physical health and prosperity of soul might go hand in
hand (3 John 2). And there is a sense in which the connection is still
true, even though our blessings now are spiritual (Ephesians 1:3)
rather than temporal. Where physical health does not accompany
spiritual health, we may be assured it is because God our Father is
working out some hidden purpose of blessing. But we are always free
to pray for one another that we may be healed (James 5:16).

Every form of disease healed by our Lord Jesus seems to picture
some aspect of sin, which is like a fever burning in the soul, a leprosy
polluting the whole being, a palsy making one utterly unable to take
a step toward God, and a withered hand incapable of true service.
Whatever form sin may take, Jesus can give complete deliverance
from it.

All healing is divine, whether it be by miraculous power, by
means of properly controlled physical habits, diet, and exercise, or
by direct medical treatment. It is God alone who can give renewed
health and strength. He whose power brought us into being and gave
us these marvelous bodies with all their wonderful functions, is the
only One who can keep us well or restore us from illness.

CHAPTER THREE

THE WORK OF THE DIVINE SERVANT
PART TWO

Jesus Heals on the Sabbath (Mark 3:1-6)

Again we find the Lord in conflict with the Pharisees as to the sabbath question. His declaration that the sabbath was God's gracious provision for man's comfort—never intended to add to man's burdens but rather to relieve them—had made no impression on these stern and crafty legalists.

Among the congregation in the synagogue service on this particular sabbath was a poor, helpless man with a withered hand—that is, a hand that had become paralyzed and hung uselessly by his side. Jesus' critics, knowing the compassion of His heart took it for granted that He would take an interest in this man. Instead of rejoicing in this evidence of divine love and consideration, they watched Him with jealous eyes to see if He would exercise His healing power on the sabbath. They secretly hoped He would, so they could accuse Him of violating the tradition of the elders. Such is the heart of man, even though outwardly pious and religious, when a stranger to the grace of God!

Jesus, to whom nothing was hidden and who read their minds like an open book, asked the partially paralyzed man to "stand forth." One can imagine how eagerly and hopefully he would obey, expectantly looking to Jesus for the healing of his infirmity.

Then the Lord asked the question, "Is it lawful to do good on the sabbath days, or to do evil? to save life, or to kill?" No one answered. Knowing their hypocrisy He looked on them with anger. It was holy indignation because of their pretense to honor God and their indifference to the needs of men. The hardness of their hearts grieved the tender spirit of Jesus.

He then commanded the man to stretch out his hand. At once, as he looked in faith to Jesus, he felt new life pulsating through that paralyzed limb, and he stretched it out and found it was now as well and strong as the other.

One might have thought that such an exhibition of the grace and power that was in Jesus would have filled every heart with gladness and led to praise and thanksgiving to God for having visited His people so wonderfully. But the miracle had the very opposite effect on these jealous advocates of human traditions as opposed to divine revelation. They exhibited an utter lack of conscience toward God while displaying a punctilious concern for the observance of their traditions and false conceptions of the will of God regarding the observance of the weekly sabbath. The Pharisees, stern champions of orthodoxy that they were, entered into collaboration with the Herodians, the worldly and corrupt politicians of their day. Both groups wanted to lay hold of Jesus and put Him out of the way. Thus did extremes meet then, as often since. Men of entirely opposite views agreed on the rejection of Christ and consulted each other about how He might be destroyed. Such is the inevitable evil of the natural heart in its opposition to God!

Jesus Heals Multitudes (Mark 3:7-12)

We are told that Jesus withdrew Himself and that with His disciples He returned to the shore of the sea of Galilee. Learning of His whereabouts, great crowds assembled. They came not only from Galilee itself but also from Judea, from as far southeast as Idumaea (the land of Edom), and from as far northwest as the regions of Tyre and Sidon. The fame of Jesus had spread far abroad. It was a time of expectation and speculative ferment among the Jewish people everywhere, who confidently looked for the predicted appearance of the long-desired Son of David who was to bring liberty and salvation to Israel. The hope that Jesus, the prophet from Nazareth, might be the Messiah evidently was in the hearts of the multitudes that came from near and far to hear His words and to behold His works of power.

So dense was the crowd that they pressed upon Jesus as He stood on the narrow beach. He therefore asked of one of His disciples (Peter, we know from other records) for the privilege of using his fishing boat, which was anchored offshore, as a pulpit. Standing in this little ship He addressed the people who hung avidly on His words. The hills rise from the shore in that particular section of the coast of the little inland sea like a vast amphitheater so that the voice of the speaker would be heard readily by thousands.

Many sick ones were in that crowd, and after finishing His discourse Jesus healed all who came. So great was their faith in His healing power that they stretched forth eager hands, believing that to touch even His garments would bring the deliverance for which they longed. None were disappointed. Even those possessed with demons were freed from their bondage, the evil spirits proclaiming the truth of His deity. But He did not look with favor on audible recognition from these vile powers, and so commanded them to refrain from acknowledging Him in this way.

Jesus Ordains the Twelve (Mark 3:13-21)

From among the many who had become disciples of Jesus He chose twelve who were to be intimately associated with Him. With one unhappy exception, they were destined to become His witnesses after His death and resurrection.

"He ordained twelve . . . that he might send them forth to preach." It is not men who choose or appoint themselves to be servants of Christ. He chooses and ordains His own (John 15:16). All of the twelve apostles were what we might call "hand-picked men" (even Judas), being the special objects of divine interest. Helpless in themselves, the twelve were empowered by the Lord to do mighty works in order to accredit the message they were to carry to Israel.

The name of Simon, whom the Lord surnamed Peter, stands alone in verse 16. He was in some respects the prince of the apostles. His warm, energetic nature and fervency of spirit fitted him in a special way for leadership after he was endued with the Holy Spirit at

Pentecost. His ministry, as we know, was to the Jews particularly, although it was he who also opened the door of faith to the Gentiles by proclaiming the gospel in the house of Cornelius. Jesus surnamed him "a stone."

Next in order are "James the son of Zebedee, and John the brother of James; and he surnamed them Boanerges." When Jesus gave a new name to anyone, it indicated some characteristic He saw in him or which He was to produce in him in days to come. *Boanerges* is interpreted for us as "sons of thunder." These young men were evidently of an electric disposition, easily stirred to quick judgments, and likely to be committed readily to decisive action. James was the first of the twelve to seal his testimony with his blood. John, evidently the youngest of the entire group, outlived them all, and after almost incredible suffering, died a natural death at Ephesus in the last decade of the first century of the Christian era.

Andrew was the brother of Peter, and it was the former who led the latter to Christ, as we are told in John 1:40-42. The names of Philip and Bartholomew (also called Nathanael) are linked together. They were friends before they met Jesus, and it was Philip who introduced Nathanael to the Savior. Matthew, also known as Levi, had been a tax collector in the Roman customhouse at Capernaum, but left all to follow Jesus. Of Thomas's earlier life we know nothing. He is chiefly remembered for his outspoken declaration of his doubt as to the identity of the One whom the rest declared to be the risen Christ. But when Jesus appeared a week later, Thomas was convinced and worshiped Him as his Lord and God. James and Thaddaeus (or Judas, not Iscariot) were brothers, sons of Alphaeus, and apparently cousins of Jesus. Simon the Canaanite, elsewhere distinguished as the Zealot, had belonged to a radically subversive party of Jewish patriots working secretly, and at times overtly, for the deliverance of Palestine from the Roman yoke.

The last of the list is Judas Iscariot (the man of Kerioth) who was to be doomed to eternal infamy. He seems to have been the "gentleman" of the twelve, a man of culture, appointed to be the treasurer of the little company. Judas was trusted by the rest as deserving special recognition, but he proved to be unreal and hypocritical from the very beginning. Of him Jesus said later, "One of you is a devil."

After giving us this list Mark hastened rapidly on, as it were, to tell us of the further activities of God's anointed servant. So many came to Jesus for healing and instruction that there scarcely seemed time for any physical relaxation on His part. He was kept so busy that neither He nor the twelve had leisure even to take their ordinary meals quietly and restfully. His friends—by that is meant His immediate relatives—actually feared for His mental health and, considering Him distraught, sought to dissuade Him from further service for a while at least. But He allowed none to interfere with the work He had come to do.

Jesus Warns of the Unpardonable Sin (Mark 3:22-30)

As the multitudes watched the miracles Jesus performed, certain scribes, religious leaders who had come up from Jerusalem, looked on with envy and jealousy. Observing His growing power over the minds of the populace, the leaders feared for their own prestige and authority. Even when demons departed from their victims, exorcised by His word, the scribes and Pharisees refused to believe that the Spirit of God was working in and through Jesus thus accrediting Him as the promised Messiah. Deliberately they declared, "He hath Beelzebub, and by the prince of the devils [demons] casteth he out devils [demons]"! The statement was an evidence of the utter hardness of their hearts and their complete rejection of His testimony. In declaring the work of the Holy Spirit to be that of the prince of the demons, the scribes crossed the deadline. Their hearts were hardened, and the day of repentance for them had passed.

This is what some have designated "the unpardonable sin." Actually there is no sin that is unpardonable if men repent and turn in faith to Christ. But it is possible to sin so that the conscience becomes seared as with a hot iron. Men then lose all desire to repent and are given up to strong delusion; believing a lie, they are doomed to eternal perdition. It was so with these scribes. They had refused every witness God had given to the truth as set forth in Jesus.

The Lord exposed the wickedness and foolishness of the suggestion that He had cast out demons by the aid of the prince of demons when He asked, "How can Satan cast out Satan?" And He declared that "if a kingdom be divided against itself, that kingdom cannot stand." Nor could a house so divided continue. Neither was it possible to believe that Satan would rise up against himself and seek to destroy his own kingdom. To do so would mean an end of his power over mankind.

As a strong man, Satan had held the poor victims of demon possession in bondage for years until the stronger One came to bind him with His word and so spoil his house. To refuse the Holy Spirit's testimony was to show that one allied himself completely with Satan in this great conflict. Therefore Jesus added solemnly, "Verily I say unto you, All sins shall be forgiven unto the sons of men, and blasphemies wherewith soever they shall blaspheme: but he that shall blaspheme against the Holy Ghost hath never forgiveness, but is in danger of eternal damnation." The scribes committed blasphemy by saying, "He hath an unclean spirit."

Mark 3:28-29 was never intended to torment anxious souls honestly desiring to know Christ, but the verses stand out as a blazing beacon warning of the danger of persisting in the rejection of the Spirit's testimony of Christ until the seared conscience no longer responds to the gospel message.

Jesus Introduces a New Family (Mark 3:31-35)

Even the mother of Jesus evidently had not yet fully understood the nature and destiny of her miraculously conceived Son. She and other relatives of Jesus stood on the outskirts of the crowd and sent a messenger bidding Him come to them. In His answer the Lord showed how all merely natural relationships were to be superseded by those of a spiritual character. He asked, "Who is my mother, or my brethren?" Then looking around at the eager faces of those who were listening earnestly to His words He exclaimed, "Behold my mother and my brethren! For whosoever shall do the will of God, the same is my brother, and my sister, and mother." Thus Jesus emphasized the great truth that He had told Nicodemus: "That which is born of the flesh is flesh; and that which is born of the Spirit is spirit" (John 3:6). The new birth, demonstrated by obedience to the Word, brings one into everlasting relationship to our Lord Jesus Christ.

As we continue to read about the work of the divine servant, we observe that under the guidance of the Holy Spirit Mark was not led to record the events in the life and ministry of Jesus in their exact chronological order. Rather in a beautiful moral order, Mark linked together certain facts and teachings that emphasize outstanding principles.

CHAPTER FOUR
PARABLES OF THE DIVINE SERVANT

Parable of the Sower (Mark 4:1-20)

As previously observed, the Gospel of Mark does not follow a direct chronological order in relating the works and teaching of our Lord. This portion, which corresponds to Matthew 13, gives us an account of parabolic instruction delivered by the sea of Galilee in the summer of A.D. 28, according to the most likely system of time reckoning.

The land rises gently from the particular part of the sea of Galilee where this instruction was given. As the Lord Jesus sat in the fisherman's boat His audience would be before Him, conveniently seated or standing, as in a natural amphitheater. This natural setting enabled all to hear the voice of the teacher whose message and personality had attracted them to Him. He used parables in teaching them. These parables were illustrations drawn from things with which the hearers were perfectly familiar, so that they could follow Jesus readily if they were so disposed.

Possibly even as Jesus taught them the parable of the farmer, the audience could see a man sowing seed not far away. The sower pictures Christ Himself primarily, though the application is true of every preacher of the Word. We need not be discouraged if much of the seed seems to be lost, for even when the greatest of all sowers was here, there were many who paid no attention to the words of grace that fell from His holy lips. Their hearts were utterly hard and unfeeling, like the well-trodden wayside paths.

"Some fell on stony ground, where it had not much earth." The soil in this instance may have looked fair, but it had not much depth. Underneath there was hard ground, speaking of lack of repentance before God. The seed without root soon withered away. Where there is no divine conviction there will be no lasting effects following a temporary stirring of the emotions.

"Some fell among thorns . . . and it yielded no fruit." The careful farmer is commanded to "break up your fallow ground, and sow not among thorns" (Jeremiah 4:3; Hosea 10:12). Thorns can more easily be avoided when dealing with individual souls. When addressing men in the mass, necessarily there will be many who are so occupied with worldly affairs the good seed can find little room to lodge.

"Other fell on good ground, and did yield fruit that sprang up and increased." The good ground pictures hearts prepared by God to receive the seed of the gospel, though even then all hearts do not produce alike. Much depends both on the depth of the Spirit's work of conviction before conversion and the time given to soul-cultivation afterward.

"He that hath ears to hear, let him hear." Thus with these solemn words, the Lord challenged our attention. It is easy to listen only with the outward ear and so fail to get the message into the heart. To those who had ears to hear and desired to understand the parable, Jesus readily gave a full explanation.

The disciples and others who had been pondering the story in their hearts came to Jesus privately and asked for its meaning. It was in the quiet of the evening in all probability, after the day's activities were ended, that He expounded the parable of the sower to them, assuring them that the mysteries of the kingdom of God would not be hidden from them. However, He would teach in parables without explaining their meaning to those who were content to remain in ignorance, in order that they might go on in their self-chosen path of blindness and indifference to spiritual truth. If they had no desire for instruction, they were to be left in ignorance. This was the righteous judgment of God on those who refuse to turn to Him and so find forgiveness of sins.

The expression, "the mystery of the kingdom of God," refers to the secrets concerning the coming days when the rejected King would return to Heaven. But as the principles of His kingdom were diffused through the world, a system would develop in which Christ would be recognized as the rightful King, and His Word would be acknowledged as rule. This system is the sphere of profession commonly called *Christendom*, which means literally "Christ's kingdom." In it are found those who are real and unreal, who profess subjection to His authority whether truly born of God or not.

Christ explained the parable by saying that the seed represents the word—the truth He came to proclaim. The wayside hearers are those who are utterly without exercise as to spiritual things. They hear the word with the outward ear but are so under the control of Satan (represented by the birds) that he takes away all consideration for the seed sown in their hearts.

The stony-ground hearers seem at first to give evidence of real conviction. Like Bunyan's Mr. Pliable, they are easily persuaded to make a Christian profession and just as easily turned from it when difficulties arise. They stumble because they have no root in themselves.

The thorny-ground hearers apparently receive the word with joy, but the quest for wealth and the desire for worldly advantage choke the word so that it becomes unfruitful.

The good ground hearers not only hear the word but also receive it in faith in their hearts. They bear fruit unto God, thus demonstrating the reality of their confession. It is true that all do not produce to the same degree; but all bear fruit to some extent: some thirtyfold, some sixty, and some an hundred.

In considering the work of preaching the gospel we must take into account God's blessed purpose of grace and the condition of the hearts of men to whom the message comes. To some the gospel message is of no interest. They are indifferent to it from the first and never become concerned. Some are interested for a time. Their emotions are stirred, but there is no depth of commitment. Others have a measure of concern, but they are men of double mind. They would like to make the best of both worlds, and so they never give eternal things their proper place. Others, prepared by the Spirit's convicting work, are eager to know the way of life, and so "receive with meekness the engrafted word" (James 1:21) and bring forth fruit unto God.

Parable of the Candle (Mark 4:21-25)

It is possible that in Mark 4:21-25 we have a portion of the sermon on the mount, but on the other hand we may well suppose that Jesus frequently used the same metaphors to enforce the truth of His messages. In these verses the Lord gives further instruction stressing the importance of reality in our profession of faith.

A candle or lamp is not to be hidden under a bushel (which speaks of business), nor under a bed (which suggests the love of ease), but is to be displayed on a lampstand in order that it may give light to all in the house. The meaning is clear. If we profess allegiance to Christ, we are not to allow the claims of business or selfish desires of any kind to hinder our faithful testimony to Him whom we have acknowledged as our Savior and Lord.

All unreality will be disclosed sooner or later. Nothing can be hidden from the holy all-seeing eye of the Lord, nor kept secret from Him who knows the innermost thoughts and intents of the heart. All will be revealed in the clear light of His judgment seat. Happy are we if we are among those who, having ears to hear, give heed to His words!

We are warned to be careful as to what we hear and how we judge, for we ourselves will be dealt with as we deal with others; and as we hear in faith the truth of God, our knowledge will be increased. It is a law of that kingdom that to him who uses well what he has, more will be imparted, and he who has nothing but an empty profession will, at the last, be stripped even of that.

Parables of the Kingdom of God (Mark 4:26-32)

The two parables recorded in Mark 4:26-32 are related to each other morally. These parables are also recorded in Matthew 13 though in a different order.

"So is the kingdom of God, as if a man should cast seed into the ground." Preaching the word is sowing the seed, whereby the kingdom of God in its spiritual aspect is spread throughout the world. "It pleased God by the foolishness of preaching to save them that believe" (1 Corinthians 1:21). The wonder of the new birth is just as inexplicable as the mystery of life in a seed that leads to the development of a plant. (John 3:6-8).

"First the blade, then the ear, after that the full corn in the ear." The law of growth in the natural world illustrates growth in grace and in understanding of spiritual realities. Men do not suddenly become mature saints. While we are saved in a moment when we trust the Lord Jesus, our growth is a matter of years. It is as we assimilate the truth by study of the Word, prayer, and devotion to Christ that we bear fruit to perfection.

"When the fruit is brought forth, immediately he putteth in the sickle, because the harvest is come." So the great husbandman is watching over His tilled fields (1 Corinthians 3:9) until the yield is at its best. Then He will take to Himself the fruit for which He has waited so patiently (James 5:7).

"Whereunto shall we liken the kingdom of God?" Next the Lord Jesus used an altogether different illustration to picture an aspect that the kingdom was to take on after He had gone back to the Father. In this second illustration, very different indeed from the first picture of a field of wheat, He compared the kingdom of God to a mustard seed. He said that the mustard seed is "less than all the seeds that be in the earth." It is not exactly that there are no seeds anywhere smaller than those of the mustard plant, but in a garden of herbs the mustard seed is the least of all. This tiny seed pictures the small and seemingly insignificant beginning of the kingdom of God in the world, following the ascension of the Son of man to the right hand of the Father.

"It ... shooteth out great branches." The mustard tree is the largest of all the herbs and fitly pictures the kingdom as a power to be reckoned with in the earth. In other words, the mustard tree represents that which the Lord foresaw Christendom was to become—a vast all-inclusive society where "the fowls of the air" find a hiding place. The fowls of the air are representatives of Satan and his emissaries (Matthew 13:19; Mark 4:15; Luke 8:12). They devour the good seed in the parable of the sower, and now they are seen hiding in the branches of the mustard tree. How well the Lord knew the turn that events would take! The mustard-tree growth of the professing church looks good for a time, but its evanescent character will soon be manifested.

Contrasted Views of the Kingdom. The field of wheat and the mustard tree present very different pictures of the kingdom. A field of wheat is made up of many thousands of stalks, all more or less alike, differing only in the heaviness of the heads of grain. This is what the church of God should be in the world.

The mustard tree is, in a sense, an imitation of a great world-power, such as the cedar tree of Assyria (Ezekiel 31:3-6) or the great tree of Babylon, Nebuchadnezzar (Daniel 4:10-12). In both Old Testament instances, as in this parable, the fowls of the air—the emissaries of Satan—find lodging in the branches. It might have seemed impossible that the kingdom of God could ever become like this. Yet that was what our Lord predicted, and it has come to pass throughout the centuries since.

Importance of Parables (Mark 4:33-34)

The use of parables by our Lord was for a twofold purpose. He taught many deep and important truths in this form in order to test the reality of His hearers' interest. If truly concerned, they would seek to get the meaning of the story and would become earnest inquirers. If indifferent, they would pay no further attention and would go on in their careless way, hardening their hearts against the truth (Matthew 13:11-15; Luke 8:10). Those whose consciences were exercised would find that these vivid illustrations fixed in their minds the great truths that Jesus taught, making an indelible impression on them (Matthew 13:16-17).

Our Lord was the prince of preachers, and we are told that "without a parable spake he not unto them" (Matthew 13:34). The human mind is so constructed that it receives instruction far more readily through apt illustrations than just by the setting forth of either arguments or definitions. Spurgeon said it well: "The sermon is the house; the illustrations are the windows that let the light in." Those who depend entirely on abstract truth to reach the hearts and consciences of their hearers are far more likely to fail to accomplish their desires than those who brighten up their discourses by relating appropriate and enlightening incidents. In teaching, as in all else, Jesus Christ is our great exemplar. His early followers, whose utterances and letters are recorded in the New Testament, used the same method.

The parables of the Lord Jesus Christ are remarkable for their fidelity to nature and to human life. He drew His illustrations from those things with which His hearers were thoroughly familiar, so that they could understand Him readily. The illustrations and the related lessons would be fixed in their minds if there was a real desire to know that truth which makes free (John 8:32).

Jesus always took into account the moral and spiritual conditions of His hearers and gave the word as suited to each group. He used illustrations of the most clear and yet simple character. If His hearers showed any further interest He was glad to explain the meaning of any similitude that His hearers could not comprehend. He ever ministered to the needs of men. He never sought to charm or allure by "great swelling words," as do the representatives of evil systems. He used language that was easy to understand and was ever prepared to instruct any seeking soul. In all this He was the master preacher, an example to all who seek to serve Him by proclaiming His Word.

Power over Creation (Mark 4:35-41)

When Jesus had finished teaching by parables and as evening was approaching, He said, "Let us pass over unto the other side." All was settled in His mind. He did not suggest that His disciples attempt to reach the other side of the lake, which was the country of the Gadarenes (5:1), but He spoke definitely of actually crossing over. If they had remembered these words later, they would have known that no storm could alter His plans.

"They took him even as he was in the ship." He had been healing and teaching all day and no doubt was physically very weary as they received Him into the boat that was to carry Him across the lake. Note that "other little ships" were also with them.

"There arose a great storm of wind, and the waves beat into the ship." To the natural eye, conditions had become very critical. But the Lord Jesus Christ slept in peace as the storm raged. In their terror the disciples turned instinctively to the Lord Jesus and roused Him from His slumber with their cry of distress. Of course He cared, but they were as safe in the storm as on a smooth sea when He was in the ship with them.

In a quiet display of His creatorial authority He commanded the wind to die down and the angry waves, which were leaping about the vessel like mad dogs, to be "muzzled," as the command has been translated. Instantly the elements obeyed their Master, and the storm subsided. Even so He speaks today to troubled hearts and tempest-driven lives!

"Why are ye so fearful? how is it that ye have no faith?" It was as though Jesus would call the minds of His disciples back to the words He had spoken before they began their voyage. He had declared they were to pass over to the other side—not be drowned in the midst of the sea. This should have been enough to quiet their fears, and would have been, had there been real faith in His words. The disciples did not yet understand the mystery of His person, and so they questioned one another in perplexity as to His actual identity. All nature acknowledged His power. Could He then be other than God incarnate?

Who raised the storm? Was the raising of the tempest that evening on the sea of Galilee simply a natural phenomenon, or was it of definite Satanic origin? It would seem that it was an effort on the part of the adversary to destroy the Lord Jesus Christ before He could fulfill His mission. But just as when the people of Nazareth tried to shove Him over the cliff and kill Him but were unable to effect their purpose (Luke 4:28-30), so in this instance Satan was again foiled. He had no power to take the life of the Son of God. That life could be laid down only voluntarily by Christ Himself in accordance with the Father's will (John 10:17-18).

The Miracles of Jesus Christ. Rationalists and rationalizing professors of Christianity are fond of trying to explain on purely natural grounds the remarkable things credited to the Lord Jesus in the Gospels. A sample of this kind of reasoning is found in a widely-read book, *The Nazarene.* But the clear purpose of the Holy Spirit in recording these wonders was to show us that He who so marvelously healed and helped suffering humanity was God Himself come down to earth as man. No far-fetched explanations are needed if we consider who it was who did these things. All were perfectly normal manifestations of divine power at work in response to the needs of men. To deny the miracles is but an effort to belittle Him who performed them.

Jesus Christ our Lord is Master of all circumstances and sufficient for every emergency. Winds and waves obey Him; demons flee before Him; disease and death are destroyed when He appears. Nothing can withstand His power. He has all authority in Heaven and on earth. And the wonderful thing for us to know is that He is our Savior and Redeemer. We who have trusted Him are directed now to cast every care on Him because He cares for us (1 Peter 5:7). Difficulties are but opportunities for Him to display His power. Emergencies give us the privilege of proving His loving interest in us as we confide in His grace and count on His might.

CHAPTER FIVE

THE SERVANT CONTINUES HIS HEALING MINISTRY

Jesus Delivers the Demon-Possessed (Mark 5:1-20)

Crossing the sea of Galilee Jesus and His disciples entered the forbidding land of Gadara. A mixed multitude lived in Gadara, many of whom were engaged in what was considered by the stricter Jews as an illegal business, that of raising swine for the tables of the Gentiles.

On the high plateau above the shore near where the boat landed was a graveyard, or a place of many rock-hewn tombs. In and among the tombs lived a demoniac of violent character, a wild untamable man, made such by the evil powers that possessed him. He had terrorized the entire countryside for a long time. Though often captured and bound with fetters and chains, he had snapped his bonds as with superhuman might and thus freed himself from all control. Day and night his strange, weird cry could be heard as he roamed about on the mountains, cutting himself with stones and shrieking in his fearful agony. It is a terrible picture of a man completely dominated by Satan.

But he was soon to know the delivering power of Jesus. When he saw the Lord at a great distance, he came running toward Him and prostrated himself before Him. He cried with a loud voice, "What have I to do with thee, Jesus, thou Son of the most high God? I adjure thee by God that thou torment me not." Though the lips of the man moved, it was the voice of the demons that spoke. These evil spirits recognized Jesus at once and needed none to tell them the mystery of His nature. The Lord had already commanded the demon to come out of the man. Then He asked him his name. The answer was an astonishing one: "My name is Legion: for we are many." This indicated that not one alone but a vast number of evil spirits lived in the wretched man who had so terrorized his neighborhood.

Then came a strange request and more strangely still, the Lord complied. The request was that the demons (who apparently dread being disembodied completely) be permitted to enter a herd of swine feeding nearby. Leaving the body of the man, they then entered into the swine. The alarmed creatures, maddened and uncontrollable, rushed violently down a steep hill into the sea and were drowned. We need not attempt to explain this strange phenomenon, but we can reflect on the possibilities of evil when we realize that one man could hold more evil spirits than two thousand hogs could!

The freed man, once so wild and fierce, now in his right mind became gentle and quiet. Covering his formerly naked body with clothing, he took his place in adoring love and gratitude at the feet of Jesus.

Having been apprised by the herders of what had taken place, the owners of the swine came out to see for themselves. Instead of rejoicing because the demoniac was healed, they were angry over the loss of the unclean beasts which constituted their wealth. Because they looked upon Jesus as the cause of the disaster, they asked Him to depart out of their coasts.

The demoniac had been delivered in a very wonderful way from a terrible state of bondage and distress. In the gratitude of his heart he longed to leave all and go forth with the Lord Jesus as others had done. It was he who took the initiative. But it was not the will of the Lord that this man should be numbered among the twelve or even the seventy. His sphere of service was to be at home in the place where he was so well known. His witness for Christ there would count for more than if he traveled farther afield.

"He...began to publish in Decapolis how great things Jesus had done for him." *Decapolis* ("ten cities") was the name given to a group of villages on the eastern side of the sea of Galilee, the very towns from which the people had come who begged Jesus to depart out of their coasts. Through this man's testimony that attitude was changed. When Jesus again visited that district He was welcomed in a very definite manner (Mark 7:31).

Jesus Heals the Incurable (Mark 5:21-34)

From Gadara the Lord and His apostles crossed over the water to Capernaum. Here many were waiting for Him. As He began to teach them, Jairus, one of the rulers of the synagogue, fell down at the feet of Jesus and pled with Him to come to his home to heal his little daughter who lay at the point of death. Acceding readily to the troubled father's request, the Lord accompanied him to the house. A great multitude followed in the way.

As they moved along, a poor afflicted woman joined the company. She had suffered from a hemorrhage for twelve years. Mark told us that she had suffered many things of many physicians and had spent all her living in the vain effort to obtain healing, but all her efforts had failed. She was no better but rather worse. Anyone who is at all familiar with the accepted remedies which were once supposed to be of value in treating such a disease can well understand Mark's almost ironical expression. No one could use those abominable remedies without suffering; yet they were powerless to cure or even give temporary relief.

Hope sprang up in the sick woman's heart when she heard of Jesus. She exclaimed, "If I may touch but his clothes, I shall be whole." Pressing through the crowd she reached forth an eager, trembling hand, and the moment she touched His robe she knew the work was done. She felt in her body that she was healed of that plague.

Jesus immediately stopped, and looking about, inquired, "Who touched my clothes?" He desired her to confess before all the miracle that had been performed in response to her faith. The disciples actually started to reprove their Master as they reminded Him that a great crowd was pressing on Him. Why then should He inquire who had touched Him? They did not sense the difference between crowding Him and touching Him in faith.

Seeing she could not be hidden, the woman came forward, fell down before Him, and told Him why she had been so bold and what the effect had been. Jesus rejoiced in her confidence in His grace and power. Comforting her, He said, "Daughter, thy faith hath made thee whole; go in peace, and be whole of thy plague." Then He continued on His way to the ruler's house.

Jesus Raises the Dead (Mark 5:35-43)

Before Jesus and Jairus reached the house, messengers came bidding Jairus refrain from troubling the Master any further. It was now too late to heal the child, they reported, for she was already dead. But Jesus, reassuring the distressed father, said, "Be not afraid, only believe." What comforting words were these at such a time! Who but He, who was the Lord of life, could or would have uttered them when all hope seemed gone and death had intervened already? When we are at the end of all natural resources, the same blessed words come home to our hearts to give peace and confidence today.

"He suffered no man to follow him, save Peter, and James, and John." These three formed the inner circle of His chosen ones. Later they were with Him on the mount when He was transfigured (Mark 9:2) and they were with Him again in the garden of Gethsemane (Mark 14:32-33).

"He cometh to the house . . . seeth the tumult, and them that wept and wailed greatly." The Lord Jesus Christ took notice of it all. Much of the mourning was professional, and for that He had only contempt. But Jesus had deep and tender compassion for the parents' grief, and He was soon to change their sorrow into joy. He rebuked the hired mourners, whose loud outcries indicated no real sense of loss on their part. And besides, as all live unto Him, He could declare with absolute truthfulness, "The damsel is not dead, but sleepeth." He had come to awaken her from her sleep. To the mourners He was but a charlatan pretending to powers He did not possess. But He was soon to demonstrate the contrary. Banishing all from the house except the parents and His three chosen disciples, He entered the chamber of death to rob it of its prey.

"He took the damsel by the hand, and said unto her, Talitha cumi." He spoke in Aramaic, the language of His childhood in Nazareth.

The words are interpreted for us, "Damsel, I say unto thee, arise" (literally, "Little lamb, wake up"). There was instant response. To their joy and amazement, the parents beheld the color come again into the pale cheeks as their darling sprang from the couch and came to their arms. She was about twelve years of age and her immediate deliverance from death amazed all who beheld her.

This manifestation of our Lord's power over death made a great stir among the people, but Jesus charged them not to blazon it abroad. He had no desire to be hailed simply as a great wonderworker. His message was more important than His miracles, and He would not have attention focused on the latter to the neglect of the former. What He did was out of regard for Jairus and his wife. The newly-awakened one needed nourishment, so He "commanded that something should be given her to eat." Nothing could be more fitting nor furnish clearer proof of the reality of the miracle accomplished in her body.

Conclusion

The first division of the Gospel of Mark comes to a conclusion with Mark 5. Throughout the first division we see Jehovah's Servant ministering in grace to the needs of men as He proclaimed the love of the Father. But He was constantly opposed and increasingly rejected by the leaders in Israel, though the common people heard Him gladly. However, not even a great many of these common people received Him in faith and acknowledged Jesus as their rightful Lord.

The four distinct incidents in the gracious ministry of our Lord recorded in the last part of Mark 4 and in Mark 5, all bear witness to the deity of Him who had stooped in grace to take the servant's place. In the first incident (4:35-41) we see His power over nature, eliciting the cry of amazement from His disciples, "What manner of man is this…?"

The second scene depicts His power over Satan, as evidenced in the deliverance of the demoniac. He would have remained in Christ's company, but was sent back to bear witness among his own people to the deliverance that the Lord had brought. Though at the time the inhabitants of that district, distressed over the loss of their swine, begged the Lord Jesus to depart out of their coasts, we learn in a later passage that they received Him gladly when He came the second time into that same region (see Mark 5:20 and 7:31-37). Who can doubt that the redeemed man's testimony had helped to change their attitude?

The stories of the healing of the woman who had an issue of blood and the raising of Jairus's daughter are intertwined in Mark 5:21-43 and demonstrate the Savior's power over disease and death. The poor, sick woman who "had suffered many things of many physicians," but was worse off after their treatments than before, found in this great physician One who understood her case thoroughly. He healed her instantly when in faith she touched the blue border of His garment (Matthew 9:20). (As a true Israelite, Jesus Christ undoubtedly obeyed to the letter the commandment found in Numbers 15:38.)

The little dead child was beyond all human help, but when He who is the resurrection and the life (John 11:25) entered the room where the body of the maiden was laid out in preparation for burial, Death fled before Him and the daughter was restored to her parents.

The three recorded instances in which Christ raised the dead are very suggestive. All people are dead in sin, and only He can give life. Whether it be a child in her comparative innocence (Mark 5:35-43), a young man in his youthful vigor (as in the case of the son of the widow of Nain, Luke 7:11-17); or one in his maturity (like Lazarus, who had been dead four days and whose body was in process of corruption, John 11:1-44)—all needed the life that Christ alone could give, and He proved Himself sufficient for each case.

CHAPTER SIX
OPPOSITION DEVELOPS

The Prophet Without Honor (Mark 6:1-6)

The mighty works of Jesus had made a distinct impression on the mass of the people who heard Him with eagerness. But few of the more cultured and outwardly religious classes were prepared to acknowledge Him as the promised Servant of Jehovah who was to deliver Israel. Instead of assenting to His Messianic claims, they became suspicious of Him as an impostor and arrayed themselves in definite opposition to Him, even going so far as to seek some method whereby they might destroy Him. This attitude is apparent in Mark 6 and becomes increasingly prominent in Mark 7–10.

Jesus found opposition in His own neighborhood. As Mark 6 opens we see Him in the city of Nazareth and the region roundabout, where He had lived as a child and as a young man.

Jesus entered the synagogue where He must often have met with His fellow townsmen in the years gone by. There He taught in such a way that the people were astonished since they knew He was not a product of any of the rabbinical schools, but had lived among them as a carpenter. His family was well known to them. They spoke of Him as the son of Mary and the brother of James, Joses, Juda, and Simon. They also mentioned "his sisters." This seems to prove conclusively that Mary had other children after the birth of Jesus, her firstborn (Matthew 1:25). Romanists deny this and speak of Mary as "ever virgin." They insist that the brothers and sisters here mentioned must have been children of Joseph by a former marriage, or possibly were cousins of Jesus. But this appears to be a mere subterfuge to evade the truth that Mary actually became the wife of Joseph.

Jesus answered His skeptical neighbors by saying, "A prophet is not without honour, but in his own country, and among his own kin, and in his own house."

So intense was their incredulity that we are told He could do no mighty work there, although He healed a few sick ones who came to Him in their distress. God works in response to faith. Unbelief ties the hands of omnipotence, except in judgment, and the hour for judgment had not yet come.

Jesus marveled that those who had known Him so well should be so distrustful of Him and even opposed to Him. Luke's account tells us that they actually tried to hurl Him over the cliff on which the city was built. But passing through the midst of them, He went His way, grieved at their hardness of heart.

Jesus Sends Out His Couriers (Mark 6:7-13)

The twelve whom Jesus had already chosen to be with Him were now commissioned to go through the villages of Galilee to proclaim the gospel of the kingdom. The disciples were to call the people to repentance, so that they would be prepared to receive the King when He was revealed to them. Jesus sent the disciples out two by two that they might labor together in fellowship and testimony. He empowered them to heal the sick and cast out demons, thus accrediting them as His representatives.

Because the disciples were going to their own people Israel, and on account of the urgency of their errand, He told them to take nothing for their journey except a pilgrim staff—no scrips, (provision bags), no provisions, no money in their purses. They were to be shod with sandals and not to be encumbered with two cloaks.

When the disciples entered a city or village they were to accept hospitality from whoever offered it, and were to remain in that host's house, if welcome, until they left town. There was to be no ground for the suspicion that they were seeking personal comfort or special recognition. Where the disciples were not received, they were to shake off the dust from beneath their feet as a testimony against those who spurned their message. For such there could be nothing but judgment ahead—a judgment far worse than that which fell on Sodom and Gomorrha.

Following their Master's instructions they went out preaching that men should repent—that is, change their attitude toward God. Repentance involves a new attitude in regard to self and sin. They also cast out demons and healed many who were sick. It is of interest to note that they anointed with oil those who came for healing, as commanded in the Epistle of James. This is the only other instance where this particular method is mentioned in connection with physical healing. Some have thought the oil was used as a remedy. The medicinal use of oil was an acceptable practice as indicated in the story of the good Samaritan who poured oil and wine into the wounds of the one who was left in a dying condition on the Jericho road. But oil is also the accepted symbol of the Holy Spirit, and it seems more likely that the anointing was intended to indicate the Spirit's gracious action of healing in answer to the prayer of faith.

Herod Beheads John the Baptist (Mark 6:14-29)

The account of godless Herod's perfidious treatment of John, the forerunner of Jesus, fills one's whole soul with horror, and yet it is but a portrayal of the capability of man's natural heart. When Herod heard of the miracles wrought by Jesus, his guilty conscience was aroused, and he said that John the Baptist had risen from the dead, and that therefore these mighty works were performed by him. Others thought He must be the promised Elijah who, according to Malachi, was to come to call Israel to repentance before the great and dreadful day of the Lord. Others said He was a prophet, or possibly one of the older prophets come back to life. But Herod was for the time being convinced that Jesus was none other than John revived. Herod lived over again the scene in which he had been reproved for Herodias' sake. He was haunted by the imprisonment and finally the decapitation of the desert preacher. When Herod thought of the infamous treatment he had meted out to the fearless proclaimer of man's need to repent, he knew he had been guilty of a terrible crime before God and man.

Herod had been interested in John's message at first, and had sent for him in order that he might hear for himself the desert preacher. As long as John dealt with the gospel of the kingdom, his royal but corrupt auditor listened with some measure of attention. But when the Baptist dared to rebuke the crafty and licentious monarch for his incestuous relations with his brother Philip's wife, the king's ire was stirred. He endeavored to silence his reprover by shutting him up in a gloomy prison, probably Machaerus on the cliffs overlooking the Dead Sea. There John was left to languish. (In Matthew 11:2-3 we read that while John was in prison he sent two of his disciples to question whether Jesus could indeed be the promised Messiah. This may have been done to satisfy John's own doubts or to establish the faith of his disciples.)

While John was in prison Herod observed his birthday by inviting guests to a feast. The celebration was turned into a vile oriental orgy of drunkenness and debauchery. The daughter of Herodias was called in to add to the carnal enjoyment of the military and civilian chiefs and other dignitaries who were present. Her undoubtedly voluptuous dance so delighted the spectators that Herod impulsively offered the girl any favor up to half his kingdom as a reward for her performance.

Moved by her wicked mother, she asked for the head of John the Baptist on a charger (a large platter). Herodias fully exemplified the poet's line, "Hell hath no fury like a woman scorned." Shocked by her request the king would have refused compliance, but for his oath's sake given before all those present he did not dare refuse lest he lose face and become an object of ridicule to his retainers. After all, it would be only one more murder added to the many of which he was guilty already! So he at once sent an executioner to decapitate the prophet and bring his gory head as requested to the dancer, who in turn gave it to her mother.

One can imagine how Herodias gloated over the gruesome object as she realized those cold lips would never again charge her with adultery or other sins. But she had not seen the last of John the Baptist. In the day of judgment he will rise up to condemn her because of her callous indifference to the call to repentance.

When John's disciples learned what had taken place they came and took the body of their master and gave it decent burial. In

Matthew 14:12 we read that they "went and told Jesus," who entered into their great grief in tenderest sympathy.

Jesus Feeds the Five Thousand (Mark 6:30-44)

In this section of Mark we read of the return of the twelve from their preaching tour and the report they gave to Jesus. The apostles, with exuberant spirit, gathered around their Lord and told Him all that they had done and what they had taught as they went about visiting the villages of Galilee. He saw that they were perhaps too much occupied with their own success and that they were somewhat overwrought because of the strain under which they had been. So He invited them to leave the multitudes and retire to a quiet country place and "rest a while." How much His servants need such seasons of quiet in company with Him! So they departed into a desert place—that is, a place in the open country away from any city or town, where they might obtain the physical recuperation and mental quiet that they needed so much. If we all took time for more such occasions, nervous breakdowns and heart attacks would not be so common among the servants of Christ.

Just how long the little company enjoyed the privacy and restfulness of their time of retirement we are not told. But some people who saw the direction the group had taken carried the news to others, and soon a great crowd came together out of all the nearby cities and gathered about Jesus. He could not turn them away nor refuse to minister to them. To Him they were as sheep not having a shepherd, and His great heart was moved with compassion toward them, so that He began at once to teach them many things. With unwearied zeal He instructed them throughout all that day, seeking to make known to them the things concerning the kingdom of God.

The disciples became concerned about the hungry people who had been with the Lord Jesus all day. Many of them were far from their homes. The night was coming on, and it seemed to be both kind and prudent to urge them to return at once to their different homes. If they were to secure proper food before the night fell they should hurry away, for there was no provision made for them in that desert place, so far as the disciples could see.

Our Lord's command to feed the crowd must have astonished His disciples. They had nothing to share with others, and they knew not where or how to obtain food in that secluded place. It was His desire to have the disciples consider the need of the people and their responsibility in regard to it, even as today He would have us be concerned about the spiritual dearth all about us and our responsibility to do our part in meeting its demands. We are all too quick to measure God's ability to meet our needs by that which our eyes can see; instead we should remember that we are dealing with One who created a universe from nothing and sustains it by the word of His power.

"How many loaves have ye?" We know from the other records that Andrew discovered a lad with five of the flat loaves to which the people were accustomed and two small fishes (John 6:8-9). Someone has suggested that it was the boy's own lunch—all of which he gave up that others might be fed. Little as it was, Jesus Christ could use it in a large way. In our emergencies we generally ask "Whence?" and "How?" forgetting that nothing is too hard for the Lord. He who multiplies the seed sown in the ground can take the little we bring and make it sufficient to meet the needs of many.

With authority the Savior ordered that the multitude should sit down in groups on the green grass where all could be properly served. His command was obeyed. They sat down, doubtless wondering what would happen next and questioning why He had hindered their hasty return to their homes. Our Lord's command to make the men sit down was significant. Seated on the ground, all are practically on one common level. Distinctions of stature disappear. It was the "no difference" doctrine acted out.

Receiving the food from the hands of Andrew or of the expectant lad, the Lord Jesus gave thanks and began to break the bread and divide the fishes, handing supplies to the disciples. They in turn passed them out to the hungry folk who looked on wonderingly. When the Lord Jesus broke the bread and gave to His disciples that they might pass it on to the multitude, no one would be excused if he went away hungry. So today, as we offer the living bread to hungry souls, none need go without eternal blessing.

There proved to be an abundant supply for all. None was disappointed. No one ever need go hungry from the table that the Lord

Jesus Christ spreads. Not only were all satisfied, but when the meal was over there were as many basketsful left as there were disciples. And the twelve had wondered where food could be procured for so many!

"They that did eat...were about five thousand men." Matthew 14:21 adds, "Beside women and children." So actually the number was even more than five thousand, though doubtless not many women and children would be out in the desert to hear the great teacher that day.

Long centuries before He came into the world, it was written of the promised Messiah, "I will satisfy her poor with bread" (Psalm 132:15) and "He shall feed his flock like a shepherd" (Isaiah 40:11). The feeding of the multitudes on two separate occasions must have recalled these prophecies to the minds of the people and caused them to wonder whether Jesus Christ might not be the One whose coming had been so long foretold.

When God brought Israel out of Egypt He spread for them a table in the wilderness (Psalm 78:19). The Lord Jesus gave the hungry crowds, who had followed and listened to Him all day long, an example of the same omnipotent power. It is pitiable to note how unbelieving critics attempt to discredit these testimonies of our Lord's creatorial glory. They insinuate that it was just a case of each one sharing his lunch with neighbors who had forgotten to bring any—so that as all ate together it seemed to them as though the food had been multiplied in a marvelous manner! Scripture tells us that "at the mouth of two...or...three witnesses, shall the matter be established" (Deuteronomy 19:15). Strikingly enough, the first of these miracles is one of the few given by each of the four evangelists. These men, whose integrity cannot be questioned, were either present on the occasion depicted or had been accurately informed by others. All four Gospel writers described the feeding as a supernatural occurrence. Christ, who multiplies the corn on a thousand hillsides and the fishes in all the seas, did in a few moments what is ordinarily accomplished through His divine power and wisdom in weeks or months of time.

By meeting the needs of the body, Christ taught the multitudes the compassion of God and His ability to meet every need of the soul. We shall find as we seek to serve our blessed Lord that the more we pass on to others, the more we have left for ourselves.

It never was loving that emptied a heart,
Nor giving that emptied a purse.

Jesus Walks on the Sea (Mark 6:45-56)

We have next a very striking dispensational picture of what the disciples of Christ would have to endure on the stormy sea of time while the Lord is interceding for them above.

After the feeding of the multitude Jesus directed His disciples to cross the lake. He did not go with them; but when they had left He went up into a mountain in order to be alone with His Father, to commune with Him in prayer.

"The ship was in the midst of the sea." But it was under His eye, and His heart was concerned about His disciples who were laboring hard, toiling in rowing. The wind was contrary to them as they sought to reach their intended destination. Another has pointed out that the word here rendered "toiling" (Mark 6:48, KJV) is the same as that translated "vexed" in 2 Peter 2:8, KJV. The word implies more than tense muscular activity. The disciples were in real mental distress and anxiety. They feared their boat might be swamped and they themselves drowned in the raging seas that threatened to engulf them. Possibly they were also vexed with one another and inclined to blame each other for the precarious condition in which they found themselves. What a picture this is of the state in which believers are found so often in their conflicts with circumstances during the physical absence of the Lord Jesus from this world!

How little the disciples realized as they struggled against wind and wave that all the time the eye of their Lord was on them and that His heart was concerned about them. And how easily we forget as we "wrestle on toward heaven" (as Rutherford put it), that our great high priest is ever looking down on us and making continual intercession for us!

As the earliest streaks of dawn were seen across the horizon "about the fourth watch of the night," which was what we would call from 3:00 - 6:00 a.m., Jesus came down from the mount and walked on the sea toward the disciples. Apparently He was about to pass them by when the frightened disciples, terrified because they thought Him to be a ghost, cried out in alarm. He revealed Himself to them saying, "Be of good cheer: it is I; be not afraid."

Astonished beyond measure they received Him into the ship and immediately the wind ceased. Details are given elsewhere that are omitted purposely here so that our attention may be focused on the fact that His coming to them brought an end to the storm. So will it be when He returns for His own.

The disciples were amazed at what had taken place. How quickly they forgot the evidence of His creatorial power in the multiplication of the loaves and fishes. They wondered in themselves concerning the mystery of our Lord's personality.

Safely reaching the shores of Gennesaret at last, they had hardly left their boat before the people began coming to Jesus from all that district. He could not hide: His fame had preceded Him. So they came bringing the sick in beds, beseeching Him to heal them. As He moved about from village to village, from city to city, and even out in the open country, He was besieged by the crowds. They brought sick friends and relatives, begging that they might be permitted to touch even the border of His garment; and we are told that "as many as touched him were made whole." God incarnate was walking about in the midst of His people, and it was His delight to relieve their sufferings and to cure them of their diseases. His saving-health was revealed wherever He went. Yet all this failed to convince the leaders that their long-waited-for Messiah had come to deliver them.

The next chapter tells of developing opposition that was to find its culmination in the cross.

CHAPTER SEVEN

TRADITION VERSUS REVELATION

Jesus Condemns the Traditions of the Pharisees (Mark 7:1-13)

To the spiritual mind it is a question of unceasing wonder that men should be so ready to follow and even fearlessly contend for the authority of human traditions, while they are just as ready to ignore the plain teachings of the Word of God. On many occasions we find our blessed Lord coming into conflict with the prejudices of those in Israel who exalted tradition to a level with revelation, and in some instances, to a higher level.

In Mark 7 we find our Lord dealing directly with the Pharisees' exaltation of human tradition. Mark 7:1-8 has to do with the question of eating with unwashed, or literally, unbaptized hands. Certain of the Pharisees and scribes who were ever on the watch for something with which they might find fault in the words or behavior of Jesus and His disciples, noticed that some of the disciples ate bread with what they considered defiled hands. This was an unlawful practice according to a tradition that had been handed down from early days. The more rigid Pharisees went through a long process, not only of cleansing the hands from any uncleanness but also of ceremonial washing, before they would eat. We are told in the fourth verse that "when they come from the market, except they wash [or baptize], they eat not." This is one of the many baptisms referred to in Hebrews 9:10. The word translated "washings" there is really "baptisms." Many other similar rites were observed in the cleansing of drinking vessels, dishes, and tables.

The observant legalists came directly to Jesus, and inquired why His disciples did not wash according to the tradition of the elders, but ate bread with unbaptized hands. Observe, it was not a question of behavior contrary to the Word of God but behavior contrary to mere human tradition.

In reply our Lord referred to the words of the prophet Isaiah: "Esaias prophesied of you hypocrites." This was strong language! A hypocrite is a man with a second face—really an actor, for the Greek actors appeared on the stage wearing masks in order to represent various parts and personalities. The Lord knew that while these hypocritical questioners were punctilious about such matters as ceremonial cleansing, they were careless in regard to laws definitely commanded by God and therefore carrying far greater weight. Jesus reminded the Pharisees that Isaiah had written of them, "This people honoureth me with their lips, but their heart is far from me. Howbeit in vain do they worship me, teaching for doctrines the commandments of men" (Mark 7:6-7). There is something very important here that we do well to take to heart. It is always a great mistake for those who profess to be servants of God to observe forms and ceremonial rites and traditions that have no Scriptural basis. Such traditions may seem innocent enough to begin with, but little by little they will usurp the place of the Word of God over the consciences of those who follow them, and this is most dangerous.

We are told in 2 Timothy 3:16-17 that "all scripture is given by inspiration of God, and is profitable for doctrine, for reproof, for correction, for instruction in righteousness: That the man of God may be perfect, throughly [or thoroughly] furnished unto all good works." If Scripture carefully studied and obeyed will equip a man of God to do all good works, then it should be clear that nothing is worthy to be counted a good work in the sight of God if the action is not authorized by Scripture. The recognition of this principle would save us from a great deal of folly and worthless labor in connection with the things of God. The Lord applied the words of Isaiah 29:13 to the critics of His disciples by telling them that they themselves laid aside the commandment of God and substituted human traditions such as those dealing with ceremonial cleansing. He added, "Many other such like things ye do."

Many Romanists and Protestants alike exalt tradition, directly or indirectly, to the level of Holy Scripture or even above it. How we need to get back to the place of teaching the Word of God! We need to inquire, "What saith the scripture?" when questions as to methods and teachings arise. For anything that is contrary to God's revelation can never be looked on with favor by Him, however much good it seems to accomplish.

In so writing I would not for one moment ignore the fact that Scripture itself gives considerable latitude in regard to methods of reaching the lost and seeking to help believers. The apostle Paul declared, "I am made all things to all men, that I might by all means save some" (1 Corinthians 9:22). What I would stress is the serious mistake of substituting human authority for divine authority. We need to be sure that not only our doctrines, but also our practical ways are in accordance with the Scriptures. This alone is the path of safety.

Continuing His discourse the Lord pointed out how these Pharisees ignored the plain teaching of the Word while giving full authority to tradition. Observe how strongly He speaks in Mark 7:9: "Full well ye reject the commandment of God, that ye may keep your own tradition." The natural heart revolts against that which is divine but readily accepts what is merely human.

Jesus then cited a very definite instance of conflict between tradition and the Scriptures. God had spoken through Moses, commanding that His people honor father and mother. The penalty of death was attached to the violation of this commandment. "He that curseth [that is, in any way harms or wrongs] father or mother, let him die the death" (Matthew 15:4). This would surely involve caring for aged parents who were unable to provide for themselves. The least that sons and daughters could do would be to share with their parents that which God had given to them, but the rabbis had declared that a man might dedicate all his possessions to God, declaring it to be Corban—that is, a gift for the maintenance of the work of the temple. If his parents were in need, he would insist that he had nothing with which he could help them because all he possessed had already been devoted to God. This was the very essence of selfishness under pretended piety; and thereby the Word of God was made of none effect through tradition. This was only one instance of the violation of God's truth by the substitution of human regulations. Jesus again added, "Many such like things do ye."

Jesus Defines the True Source of Defilement (Mark 7:14-23)

We are told that after condemning the traditions of the Pharisees, Jesus took occasion to instruct all the people in regard to the true nature of defilement. Hitherto the more conscientious an Israelite was, the more anxious and concerned he was about what he ate or drank, lest he even inadvertently take in something that was ceremonially unclean. If he did eat something considered unclean, he would be defiled and unfit to join with the congregation of the Lord when gathered together for worship in the temple. In Mark 7:14-16 our Lord laid down a great principle and emphasized a tremendous fact. Jesus declared that moral and spiritual defilement comes not from outward things such as food or drink but from within the man himself. Defilement comes from one's own heart, that heart which the prophet Jeremiah declared to be deceitful above all things and desperately wicked (Jeremiah 17:9).

It is evident that these words of the Lord astonished even His own disciples, so accustomed had they been to looking at things from the ritualistic standpoint. So when they had left the multitude and were in the house alone with Jesus, they asked Him to explain what He meant by speaking as He had done. Always ready to open up truth to sincere inquirers, He explained that outward things such as food and drink were only material: they could not affect the spirit of the man. Of course our Lord was not denying that there are hurtful and even poisonous foods that might seriously injure one physically. What He had in view here was defilement of spirit, which makes one unfit for fellowship with God. Food of any kind does not enter into the heart but passes through the digestive tract. Food makes no impression whatsoever on the soul or spirit of the one who has eaten or drunk.

"That which cometh out of the man, that defileth the man"—that is, those things which come from his heart defile him, for the heart itself is like a nest of unclean birds. "Out of the heart . . . proceed evil thoughts, adulteries, fornications, murders, Thefts, covetousness, wickedness, deceit, lasciviousness, an evil eye, blasphemy, pride, foolishness." What a list! Who can say that these things have never had any place whatever in his heart? Of course there are some to whom several of these things are thoroughly repugnant, and yet every man is capable of falling into every sin here mentioned if he but allows his mind to dwell on evil thoughts. There are men who deny the depravity of the natural man, but they might well consider the list set forth here and honestly answer the question, Have none of these things a place in my heart?

When we speak of the total depravity of the natural man, we do not mean necessarily that all men are guilty of all the sins enumerated here. We do mean that all men are by nature out of touch with God and that the capacity for all these sins is found in all their hearts.

Once when Dr. Joseph Cook was challenged as to the scripturalness of the doctrine of human depravity, he used the following illustration. He said that he was in possession of a very fine clock. It was a beautiful piece of furniture and an adornment to the room in which it was placed. The works were very expensive; the face of the clock was beautiful to look upon; the hands were of excellent workmanship; and altogether it was an admirable clock. There was only one thing wrong with it: it would not keep time. As a timepiece it was totally depraved. So it is with the natural man. He is out of touch with God. His heart is at enmity with God and from within that heart come forth many different sins. Thank God there is a remedy for this condition! David prayed, "Create in me a clean heart, O God" (Psalm 51:10), and this is what God delights to do through the new birth.

All the evil things enumerated by Jesus come from within. These defile a man. How important it is that we recognize the fact that these things naturally find lodging in the human heart, and that we judge all in the light of the cross of Christ.

Jesus Rewards the Faith of a Gentile Woman (Mark 7:24-30)

In these verses we see the grace of God going out beyond the nation of Israel. The Lord Jesus had gone into the vicinity of Tyre and Sidon—that is, in the course of His travels He had journeyed with His disciples to the northwest district of Galilee. Just beyond were the Gentile cities of Tyre and Sidon. The Lord Himself, so far as we have any record, never stepped over the border that separated Palestine from the Gentile lands, except of course when as a baby He was taken down into Egypt by His mother and Joseph, His foster father, to escape the wrath of Herod. Jesus came into the world, as Paul told us in Romans 15:8, as "a minister [or servant] of the circumcision for the truth of God, to confirm the promises made unto the fathers." While it is true that He looked forward to the time when the Gentiles might glorify God for His mercy (Romans 15:9), during His life on earth He confined His ministry to the lost sheep of the house of Israel.

But now we find Him in contact with a certain woman who was a Greek, a pure Gentile, a native of Syrophenicia. This woman had an afflicted daughter who was possessed with a demon. She had suffered terribly because of this condition. Though a stranger to the covenants of promise, the Syrophenician woman had heard of Jesus and she felt sure that He could deliver her daughter if He were willing to do so. She came, therefore, pleading that He would cast the demon out of the young girl. Elsewhere we are told that she based her plea on the fact that He was the Son of David. She had evidently learned through some of her Jewish neighbors of the Messiah who was to come in David's line, and she rightly believed Jesus to be the Messiah. So she came pleading, "Have mercy on me, O Lord, thou son of David" (Matthew 15:22). But He held His peace. As a Gentile sinner she had no claim whatever on Him as the promised Son of David. But finally, as she cried after Him, He said, "Let the children first be filled: for it is not meet to take the children's bread, and to cast it unto the dogs." This may seem to us to be a hard saying. But even as Joseph charged his brothers with being spies in order to probe their consciences (Genesis 42:8-14), so the Lord thus answered the woman in order to bring her to the place where she would recognize that her only claim to blessing was on the ground of pure grace.

She responded in a wonderful way. There was no ill-feeling on her part, as though He had insulted her or spoken to her in a discourteous manner. Humbly she answered Him, "Yes, Lord: yet the dogs [and she used a diminutive here, the little dogs] under the table eat of the children's crumbs." It was as much as to say, "Lord, I recognize the fact that I am just a poor, outcast Gentile, but give me some of the crumbs that the children of the kingdom are refusing; allow me to take the place even of a puppy under the table and so obtain mercy at Thy hand." Nothing appealed to our blessed Lord more than faith coupled with humility. He replied by saying, "Go thy way; the devil is gone out of thy daughter." She hastened to her home, doubtless with a glad heart and eager expectation. Entering the house, she found her daughter lying quietly upon the bed, the demon having left her.

Jesus Opens the Ears of the Deaf (Mark 7:31-37)

Leaving the coasts of Tyre and Sidon, Jesus crossed over the northern part of Galilee and entered into a boat, passing over the sea once more to visit Decapolis, the ten cities. It was in this region that the man from the tombs, the demoniac of Gadara, lived. After Jesus delivered him, He told him to go home and tell his friends what great things the Lord had done for him. So he spread the good news, we are told, throughout all Decapolis. Thus when Jesus returned, the people were ready to meet Him. Possibly the very ones who on the former occasion had besought Him to depart out of their coasts were among the eager crowd who came to hear His words and see His miracles.

We are told that they brought to Him one who was deaf and had a speech impediment. They begged Jesus to put His hands on him — those tender hands that had so often been lifted in blessing. At the touch of those hands disease and uncleanness had flown away. But the Lord dealt with this man in a somewhat peculiar manner. Recognizing the fact that opposition was developing, Jesus took him aside from the multitude instead of healing him openly before all the people. Jesus put His finger into his ears, and then spat and touched his tongue. We may wonder at this, but we need to remember that the humanity of our Lord Jesus Christ was absolutely holy and pure, untouched by sin or corruption of any kind. He was evidently indicating that the healing came from within His own being. Looking up to Heaven He sighed as He recognized the ravages that sin had made; and then speaking in Aramaic He said, "Ephphatha," which means, "Be opened." Immediately the man was able to hear and also to speak.

Jesus charged those that were around Him not to spread this abroad. As we have noticed before, He had no desire to gain notoriety as a wonderworker. While always ready to minister to the needs of men, His great mission was to proclaim the gospel of the kingdom as He went from place to place. But the people were so enthusiastic about what they saw of His mighty power that the more He commanded them to say nothing about it, the more they published it abroad. Surely everyone who knows Christ in any measure will gladly join with these people of Decapolis in ascribing all honor and glory to Him who has done all things well.

CHAPTER EIGHT

INTIMATIONS OF THE COMING GLORY

Jesus Feeds the Multitude Again (Mark 8:1-9)

The circumstances surrounding this miracle were similar to the occasion of some months before; yet it is evident that the disciples had forgotten—as we often do—the remarkable manifestation of divine power that they had seen at that time. The heart of Jesus Christ was touched by the need of the multitude, and His heart ever controlled His hand. For three days they had flocked about Him and paid attention to His teaching. Their food supplies had all given out and they were left with nothing to eat. He could not bear to leave them in that desolate condition. Many lived at quite a distance from the place in which they were. To go home hungry would work a real hardship on them.

"From whence can a man satisfy these men with bread here in the wilderness?" It was the expression of the unbelief in the hearts of the disciples. That they should so soon have forgotten the miraculous feeding of the five thousand would seem incredible if we did not know something of the untrustworthiness and unbelief of our own hearts.

"How many loaves have ye? And they said, Seven." The disciples were to have the privilege of sharing with others the provision they had made for their own need. This time they did not procure the food from someone else. Following the same procedure as in the previous miraculous feeding (Mark 6:30-44), the people were seated on the ground, and after giving thanks Jesus broke the bread and gave it to His disciples to distribute to the multitude.

"They had a few small fishes." Why were these not mentioned before? Could it be that they had been withheld by the doubting disciples until they saw how the bread was multiplied? Apparently the fishes were blessed separately and then distributed as the bread had been.

"They did eat, and were filled: and they took up of the broken meat...seven baskets." Again there was an overabundance. After the multitude was fed, the disciples received seven hampers of food in return for the bread and fishes they had entrusted to Jesus to dispense. The leftover food was sufficient to last a long time.

"They that had eaten were about four thousand." Again Matthew 15:38 adds, "Beside women and children."

It has often been pointed out that in the original Greek text two different kinds of baskets are indicated in the two accounts of miraculous feedings of the multitudes. In Mark 6, after the feeding of the five thousand, there were twelve handbasketsful left over. Handbaskets were such as folk carried with them when traveling on foot. In Mark 8, after the feeding of the four thousand, there were seven hampersful left over. Hampers were large baskets that were often used for carrying fish or transporting other goods.

The number of baskets left over in each miracle suggests a spiritual lesson. The number *twelve* is generally used in Scripture for administrative completeness, whereas *seven* is the number of mystical or spiritual perfection. The twelve baskets signified the abundant provision that will be enjoyed under Messiah's reign. The seven hampers tell us of the perfection of spiritual blessing when we learn that not by bread only do we live, "but by every word that proceedeth out of the mouth of God" (Matthew 4:4).

One of Jehovah's names of old was *El Shaddai*—"the God all-sufficient." Our Lord was revealing Himself as the incarnate God, abundantly able to meet every need, when He fed the multitudes who on these two occasions flocked to hear Him preach the gospel of the kingdom. His supplies are unlimited. What we need is faith to count on the riches of His mercy and to draw from His abundant store. The bread He gave pictured Himself as the bread of God come down from Heaven. If a man eat of this bread he will live forever (John 6:51).

The incident recorded in Mark 8:1-9 brings to an end one distinct phase of Christ's ministry.

Jesus Warns His Disciples (Mark 8:10-21)

Returning to the western side of the lake, in the region of Dalmanutha or Magadan, Jesus was met by some caviling Pharisees. Ignoring all the marvelous works that He had performed, they came asking for a sign from Heaven to authenticate His messiahship. We are told that Jesus sighed deeply in His spirit; His inmost being was grieved to find such unbelief and determined opposition from those who should have led the populace in the path of subjection to God and obedience to His Word. Why should they ask a sign? It was only an evidence of the state of their hearts. He declared that no sign would be given to that evil generation. They were set in their attitude of enmity against Him whom God had sent to redeem Israel.

Leaving them to their unbelief and hardness of heart, the Lord departed again to the other side of the lake—that is, to the region of Bethsaida Julias. There were two cities called Bethsaida, one on the western, and the other on the northern side of the sea of Galilee.

In their haste to leave Dalmanutha the disciples failed to replenish their store of bread. The characteristic bread of that country was flat loaves that were easily carried about. Apparently there was some expression of apprehension as to what provision they could obtain when they disembarked. The Lord took occasion to warn them, when He knew their concern, to beware of the leaven of the Pharisees and of the leaven of Herod. Conscience-smitten because of their carelessness in not having made proper provision for the needs of the group, the disciples leaped to the conclusion that Jesus was warning them not to purchase bread from the parties mentioned. But the Lord made it clear that by using the term *leaven* He was referring to the doctrines of these religious and political systems. These doctrines corrupted all who received them. The leaven of the Pharisees was hypocrisy and self-righteousness. The leaven of Herod was political chicanery and worldliness.

In order to ease the minds of the disciples as to food for their bodies Jesus reminded them of the miraculous feeding of the five thousand on one occasion and the four thousand on another. In each case there was not only abundance for all but many baskets of fragments were salvaged for future use. Why be anxious as to what one would eat on the morrow when the Creator of all things was with them? How ashamed the twelve might well have been of their doubts and fears as Jesus put the pointed question, "How is it that ye do not understand?"

Jesus Heals a Blind Man (Mark 8:22-26)

When the disciples reached Bethsaida Julias, they witnessed another evidence of the power of their Master. This miracle was of an exceptional character. So far as the record goes it is the only instance where healing was only partial at first and not instantaneous.

A blind man was brought to Jesus by friends who pleaded that He might touch the closed eyes and so give sight to the poor, afflicted one. Instead of doing this in the presence of all the people, Jesus took the blind man by the hand and led him out of the city. It was as though, realizing that many in the crowd were but curiosity seekers, He would take the man aside and minister to him alone. Jesus then put His hands on the man and asked him if he was able to see. The man exclaimed, "I see men as trees, walking." Sight was but partially restored. He could see different objects but could distinguish men from trees only by their walking. Once more Jesus placed His hands on the man's eyes and told him to look up. Now he was healed completely and he saw every man clearly.

Just why healing was not immediate we are not told—possibly because of lack of perfect faith on the part of the blind man or his friends. The work having been accomplished, Jesus dismissed the now happy man and told him not to go back into the town or tell of his healing to anyone there.

Peter Declares His Faith (Mark 8:27-30)

"Whom do men say that I am?" Jesus questioned His disciples in order to elicit from them a definite confession of His messiahship and divine sonship. As they moved about they heard many people discussing Jesus, and undoubtedly they had often debated in their own hearts the things that were said.

We remember that Herod, goaded by a guilty conscience, felt sure that Jesus was John risen from the dead. Others shared the same view. Some, remembering the prophetic declaration recorded in Malachi 4:5, thought Jesus must be the promised Elijah. Another group simply thought of Him as a new prophet who had suddenly appeared in Israel.

"Whom say ye that I am?" It is not enough to be familiar with other men's views of Christ, be they right or wrong. Our Lord's question was intended to emphasize the responsibility of individuals to know Him for themselves. Peter's answer was the result of deep conviction based on a divine revelation: "Thou art the Christ." The fuller confession given in Matthew 16:16 is a declaration of Peter's faith in Jesus both as the Messiah of Israel and the divine Son of God. He is both. In fact He could not be the Messiah (Christ) were He not the Son of God, for the Christ was the Son given and the Child born, as prophesied in Isaiah 9:6. It is to Him the Father says, "Thou art my Son; this day have I begotten thee" (Psalm 2:7).

Mark did not mention the Lord's commendation of Peter or Jesus' prophetic words concerning the building of His church upon the rock of His deity (Matthew 16:17-19). Mark also omitted Jesus' giving of the keys of the kingdom of Heaven, which Peter used on Pentecost and in Cornelius's house to admit Jews and Gentiles into the kingdom. All we are told in Mark 8 is that the disciples were not at that time to begin the work of making Jesus known to the world in His true character. They were to wait until after His death, resurrection, and ascension to God's right hand in Heaven.

Jesus Teaches of His Death and Resurrection (Mark 8:31-38)

Our Lord knew exactly what awaited Him, and told His disciples in plainest language what the order of events would be. He had come into the world to die. While His death would be the demonstration of man's bitter hatred toward God, it was also to be the supreme expression of God's love to man. His death was to be followed by the physical resurrection of the body of Jesus, the proof that redemption was accomplished so the believer might be justified from all things. The foreknowledge of Jesus may be accounted for in three ways, all in perfect harmony with each other. In the first place, though He had become man, He did not cease to be God, and therefore He knew from the beginning all things through which He was to pass. Then as man He was a student of the Word. He knew the Scriptures and came to fulfill them. So He based His predictions on the Scriptures. And lastly He was a prophet speaking under the direct control of the Holy Spirit.

"Peter took him, and began to rebuke him." Peter had just confessed Jesus as the Christ, the Son of the living God. Now he ventured to rebuke the Lord as though He were a discouraged man, speaking from the standpoint of one crushed and disappointed by the continued opposition of His foes. The Lord at once recognized in Peter's foolish though well-meant words the voice of the adversary, seeking to turn Him aside from the cross where He was to die as the supreme sacrifice for sin. His sharp rebuke silenced the blundering apostle, but neither Peter nor the rest really understood the revelation given.

Our Lord could make atonement for sin only by His sacrificial death. There was no other way. The word translated "atonement" in the Old Testament means far more than "at-one-ment," which is accepted by many as its true meaning. Thoughts of appeasement, satisfaction, substitution, redemption, pacification, and reconciliation are all involved. In the New Testament the concept of the atonement is expressed by a Greek word meaning "propitiation." Many English terms are needed to reveal all that is involved in the vicarious death of the cross. But apart from resurrection, all would be meaningless.

"Let him deny himself, and take up his cross, and follow me." A man carrying a cross was a man going out to die. The true disciple of Jesus is one who refuses the claims of self, and is ready to "die daily" for his Master's sake (1 Corinthians 15:31). To deny oneself is more than to be self-denying or unselfish. It means the utter setting aside of the self-life, that Christ alone may be seen (Galatians 2:20).

"Whosoever will save his life shall lose it." The professed follower who is concerned with his own best interest and lives to gratify his own natural desires will find out at the judgment seat of

Christ that his life has not counted for God—it is really lost. On the other hand, Jesus said, "Whosoever shall lose his life for my sake and the gospel's...shall save it." A life laid down for Christ's sake is a life saved for that day when all that has been done to glorify God and make known His gospel will be rewarded richly.

"What shall it profit a man, if he shall gain the whole world, and lose his own soul?" The Revised Version reads, "And forfeit his life." That is, present temporal gain will sink into nothingness if the soul, the real life, has been frittered away in things that do not profit. The only life that counts is that which has been lived for eternity.

"What shall a man give in exchange for his soul?" This question is generally used as though it meant, What shall a man take in exchange for his soul?" But it is the very opposite. If the soul is lost, what shall a man give to reclaim it? His case will be utterly hopeless. He cannot buy back the life that has been forfeited because of sin and selfishness.

Jesus solemnly declared that He will be ashamed in the final reckoning day of any who are ashamed of Him now. Our eternal destiny depends on our attitude toward the Lord Jesus Christ. To confess Him openly before men means eternal life and salvation. To deny or be ashamed of Him means eternal judgment and everlasting ruin.

Christ is the touchstone that will be used to test all hearts. As is our attitude to Him, so will be God's attitude to us when the day of reward shall come. Our blessed Lord laid down His life in order that He might save our souls and have us wholly for Himself. He loved the church and gave Himself for it (Ephesians 5:25). He considered no sacrifice too great in order to redeem us and make us His own. Surely then we should be prepared to go even to death in order to prove our love for Him. His death was atoning. By it we are justified when we trust in Him (Acts 13:39). Our sins are forever put away by His precious blood. We could have no part in making propitiation, but we are called upon to deny self and to lay down our lives if need be to attest our faithfulness to Him and our love for a world for which He gave Himself (1 John 4:10-11). If Christ died for all, then God saw all as dead, that they who live through faith in Him might henceforth live not unto themselves, but unto Him who died and rose again (2 Corinthians 5:14-15).

Again and again Jesus told His disciples of His approaching death and resurrection, but they seemed utterly incapable of grasping the meaning of His words. Yet His purpose for coming into the world and taking humanity into union with His deity was to die for them. Jesus sought to prepare the minds of His followers beforehand so that when they saw Him die, their faith would not fail.

All through His life Jesus had the cross before Him. He became man that He might die as our kinsman-redeemer (Leviticus 25:48) in order to bring us into life and liberty. Some time ago I read a sermon on "The Recklessness of Jesus." The preacher, while professing warm admiration for our Lord's earnestness of purpose, bewailed the sad impulsiveness that took Him to Jerusalem the last time. The preacher asserted that Jesus literally threw Himself into danger and courted the opposition of the leaders in Israel who were bent on destroying Him. How much better might it have been for the world, suggested this unconscious blasphemer, if He had remained quietly in Galilee. Jesus could have established a school for teachers in Capernaum, written a number of books, thereby enriching the religious literature of the world, and died at last in a good old age. Countless disciples, who honored and loved Him, could have been trusted to carry His instruction to the ends of the earth. One shudders at such wicked nonsense.

Had the Lord Jesus not died for our sins, there would have been no living message to carry to the world. "The Son of man came not to be ministered unto, but to minister, and to give his life a ransom for many" (Matthew 20:28). We are told that "Christ died for our sins according to the scriptures" (1 Corinthians 15:3). "Christ died"—that is history. "For our sins"—that is the central doctrine of grace. Before He left the glory that He had with the Father before the world was (John 17:5), He said, "Lo, I come to do thy will, O God" (Hebrews 10:9). The will of God to which He referred specifically was the settling of the sin question. He came to earth to put away sin by the sacrifice of Himself (Hebrews 9:26). Voluntarily He put Himself at the disposal of sinful men that this will of His Father might be carried out (John 14:31). No one took His life from Him; He laid it down of Himself (John 10:18). All was foreknown and predetermined, though this did not lessen man's guilt in rejecting Him (Acts 2:23).

CHAPTER NINE

THE PATH OF DISCIPLESHIP

PART ONE

The Transfiguration (Mark 9:1-8)

In Mark 9:1-8 we have a foreview of the glory to be revealed at the second coming of the Lord Jesus. The first verse contains what must have been to the disciples a very startling declaration. Jesus said that among those standing with Him were some who would not die until they actually had seen the kingdom of God coming in power and great glory. His words were fulfilled a week later. The apostle Peter referred to this event—the transfiguration—when he told us that the disciples had not followed cunningly devised fables when they made known the power and coming of the Lord Jesus Christ, but had been eyewitnesses of His majesty when they were with Him in the holy mount (2 Peter 1:16-17).

"He was transfigured before them." The transcendent glory of His deity shone out through the veil of His flesh. His appearance was changed in such a way as to fill His disciples with amazement and impress them with a sense of His mysterious personality. His very garments appeared to be etherealized and glowed with a brilliance no fuller could produce. The word translated "fuller" originally meant a dresser of skins or hides, but came to be applied in a wider sense to a worker in linen or other material used for apparel.

"Elias [Elijah] with Moses...were talking with Jesus." These worthies had been in paradise for many centuries. They were living, conscious, and capable of conversing with the Lord and with one another. They stand as the representatives of the law and the prophets. They also represent two classes of believers: those who will die before the Lord returns and those who will be caught up (or raptured) when He returns (John 11:25-26).

Peter was so overwhelmed with what he saw and heard that he proposed to honor the three who appeared in glory by building for them special booths. He did not realize the incongruity involved in putting even the greatest of God's servants on a level, as it were, with the Lord Jesus Himself. Moreover, he did not recognize the transitory character of the scene that enthralled him. He wanted to erect three tabernacles in order to give some permanent place of dwelling to each of the three who conversed together. How many since Peter's day have thought to honor Christ by giving special prominence to His servants—whether prophets, apostles, saints, or angels—and have never realized that in thus recognizing them as worthy of such homage they have actually dishonored the Master Himself!

"He [Peter] wist not what to say." How much better if he had been content to remain silent! But Peter was of that restless character which made him feel he must say something, and he spoke out of place and out of line with the mind of God. The Father would not have others occupying the hearts of His people in such a way as to detract from the glory that belongs to Christ alone. What seems like piety and humility is oftentimes a subtle form of pride and unbelief (Colossians 2:18-19).

"This is my beloved Son: hear him." It is Christ whom the Father delights to honor. He would have all men recognize and obey Him. When Moses and Elijah disappeared, Jesus Christ alone remained to be worshiped and adored.

This beautiful and inspiring picture of the coming kingdom is worthy of the most careful examination. Consider the various characters and note how they picture the different persons or groups who will have their places at the revelation of Jesus Christ.

First of all we see Him revealed in His glory as the center of all the Father's counsels. Then we have the two men who talked with Him of His death (Luke 9:31), which is the foundation of all our blessing and will be the theme of our praise forever (Revelation 5:9). Moses and Elijah are archetypal men. Moses had died long before, but he appeared in his resurrection body. He represents all who will die before Christ's return, but who will hear His voice and be raised in incorruptible bodies when He descends from Heaven (1 Corinthians 15:52). Elijah had been taken up to Heaven without passing through death, and so he represents all who will be "alive and remain unto the coming of the Lord" (1 Thessalonians 4:15). These people will never die at all, but will be changed in a moment and caught up to meet the Lord in the air. At His coming in glory all those represented by Moses and Elijah will be revealed with Christ. They form the heavenly side of the kingdom. On the earth there will be saints in their natural bodies. These are represented by the three apostles, who beheld the glory, but were themselves still in bodies of flesh and blood. They were all of Israel, and these will be the first to enter into the kingdom when set up on earth. The nations that have been torn and rent by Satanic power will then find deliverance, and so enter into that reign of peace and righteousness. This is suggested by what took place at the foot of the mountain (Mark 9:17-29).

Explanation of the Coming of Elijah (Mark 9:9-16)

As the little party descended from the mountain where they spent the night, which was probably mount Hermon, the Lord Jesus charged them to say nothing whatever concerning that which they had seen until after He had been raised from the dead. The resurrection was still a mystery to them. Although the Lord had spoken on several previous occasions of His dying and rising again on the third day, they could not seem to understand. As they went down the mountain they questioned one another as to what the expression "rising from the dead" could possibly mean.

Evidently they were assured in their hearts that Jesus was Messiah. But a question arose about Malachi's prophecy which declared that Elijah would be sent before the great and dreadful day of the Lord. Familiar with the Scriptures, the scribes taught the people to look not primarily for Messiah but first for Elijah, and so the disciples asked Jesus, "Why say the scribes that Elias must first come?"

Jesus declared, "Elias is indeed come, and they have done unto him whatsoever they listed, as it is written of him." The disciples understood then that He was referring to John the Baptist (Matthew 17:13). John's ministry was Elijah-like. He came denouncing sin and calling the people to repentance, that they might be in condition to receive Messiah when He appeared. Elsewhere we are told that Jesus said, "If ye will receive it, this is Elias, which was for to come" (Matthew 11:14). John the Baptist was not received by all, and his ministry did not have the effect it should have had on the entire nation because of their unbelief.

Some would suggest that there is yet to be a further fulfillment of Malachi's prophecy, and that in the days of the great tribulation after the rapture of the church another Elijah-like minister will be raised up of God to prepare the remnant of Israel to receive the anointed One. This may indeed be true.

Reaching the plain, Jesus immediately noticed a great multitude gathered about the nine disciples who had not been with Him that night in the mount. Some of the scribes were talking with them, evidently debating certain questions having to do with the possible messiahship of Jesus. When He appeared the multitude turned toward Him, and we are told that they "were greatly amazed, and running to him saluted him." Just what amazed them we may not be able to say with certainty, but the suggestion has been made that there was still something of the glory shining in His face, even as when Moses came down from the mountain after spending forty days with God. Turning to the scribes He asked them, "What question ye with them?"

Healing of the Demon-Possessed (Mark 9:17-29)

A man in the multitude spoke up and pleaded for help for his afflicted son who was possessed by a demon. The poor father's heart was torn with anguish as he told of the distressing condition under which the poor lad lived. In his desire to see his son relieved the father had brought him to the disciples. The father pleaded with them to deliver the boy, but they could not cast out the demon.

Jesus had already empowered the disciples to do that very thing, and as they moved about the cities of Galilee they had on various occasions cast out demons, but in this instance they seemed utterly powerless. Turning to them Jesus rebuked them, saying, "O faithless generation, how long shall I be with you? How long shall I suffer you?"

Then turning to the father, He said, "Bring him unto me." The lad was brought to Jesus, and when He looked upon the boy, the evil spirit that was in him immediately threw him to the ground in a convulsion—like one in an epileptic fit. The Savior looked down on the lad with compassion and asked the father, "How long is it ago since this came unto him?" The father replied, "Of a child," and looking to Jesus, he made the pitiable plea, "If thou canst do any thing, have compassion on us, and help us." It is evident that his faith was very imperfect. He believed in his heart that Jesus might be able to help, but he was not sure that He would be willing to do so.

"If thou canst believe." Jesus turned things completely around. The "if" was on the seeker's part. Where there is genuine faith "all things are possible to him that believeth." As the tears streamed from his eyes, the anxious father asserted his faith; yet recognizing its weakness, he cried for increased confidence, that the Lord might undertake on his behalf.

With a voice of authority Jesus commanded the demon to release his victim and never to control him again. So strenuous was the convulsion as the evil, malignant fiend withdrew that the lad fell to the ground as though dead, so that many supposed he was actually gone. But it proved to be the demon's last act before the boy was completely freed from his malign influence. Reaching out His hand, Jesus held that of the unconscious youth and, as He did so, consciousness and physical strength returned. To the father's joy his son came to his feet—healed and in his right mind.

Leaving the crowd the Master and His disciples entered a house, probably that of Peter, and when they were alone the disciples asked Him privately, "Why could not we cast him out?" Jesus answered, "This kind can come forth by nothing, but by prayer and fasting." Some manuscripts omit the last two words, and yet there seems to be evidence that these words should be included. Anyway, the great point the Savior made was this: no one can have power over unclean spirits unless he is in intimate touch with God.

The Definition of True Greatness (Mark 9:30-41)

Leaving Capernaum where the healing of the demon-possessed son took place, Jesus and His disciples moved on to other parts of Galilee. The Lord endeavored to avoid anything like vulgar publicity. As they walked along the roads He continued to expound the truths of the kingdom to the disciples, and once more told them of the death He was soon to die. Jesus said, "The Son of man is delivered into the hands of men, and they shall kill him; and after that he is killed, he shall rise the third day." One would have thought no language could be clearer than this, and that anyone hearing it would have comprehended that which the Lord was seeking to make so plain. But we are told in verse 32 that the disciples felt reticent about exposing their own ignorance concerning a matter of which the Lord had spoken so frequently, but whose meaning they could not understand. Doubtless the reason was that their minds were so set on the thought of the coming earthly glory that the rejection and death of Him whom they believed to be Messiah seemed incredible. (See Matthew 17:22-23 and Luke 9:43-45.)

Returning to Capernaum Jesus asked the disciples, "What was it that ye disputed among yourselves by the way?" They did not realize that their thoughts were known to Him. He did not need to hear their words to know what was in their hearts. Failing to recognize the true character of the kingdom of God, they thought of it as a place for worldly advancement. So they contended with each other as to their respective merits and likelihood of prominence when the kingdom would actually be set up.

"If any man desire to be first, the same shall be last of all, and servant of all." He who will be most highly honored in the kingdom of God is the one who seeks no honor for himself, but lays himself out for the blessing of others.

"He took a child, and set him in the midst of them." Children felt they could trust the Lord Jesus. His very grace and gentleness attracted them. So the little one came at His bidding and wonderingly took his place among the surprised disciples. The child was Christ's representative, for Christ's kingdom is one of love and lowliness. And when He is received, the Father who sent Him is received. It is in the heart of the meek and contrite that God loves to dwell (Isaiah 66:1-2).

In spite of Jesus' implied rebuke, the disciples desired to emphasize their loyalty to Christ. John spoke up and told how they had forbidden a man to cast out demons because he was not of their company. Such an attitude is common to many today who think more of sectarian affiliation than of carrying on the work of the Lord. We are all prone to overestimate the importance of our own particular group and to underrate others who do not see eye to eye with us. But the supreme test is the heart's attitude toward Christ. God is not dealing with any party to the exclusion of others. His presence, by the Spirit, is not confined to any one special company of believers, however sound they may be. He recognizes all as His children who trust His Son, whatever their associations may be, although we on our part are responsible to separate from all known evil.

"There is no man which shall do a miracle in my name, that can lightly speak evil of me." The very fact that this man acted in the name of Jesus Christ indicated his faith in Him. Where Christ's name is acknowledged, He will be loved and honored, at least in measure.

It is so easy to be sectarian in spirit. Jesus declared a great truth that we should never forget when He said, "He that is not against us is on our part." On another occasion He said, "He that is not with me is against me" (Matthew 12:30). That is positive, but in Mark 9:40 He speaks negatively. If one is not definitely arrayed against Christ then he is to be considered as on Christ's side. This is something most of us forget. But the Lord never spurns anyone who is seeking to know Him and to do His will.

"Whosoever shall give you a cup of water to drink in my name, because ye belong to Christ...shall not lose his reward." Notice that expression, "because ye belong to Christ." It is not a question of whether one belongs to our particular group, or whether he follows our ways, but whether he belongs to Christ. Whatever is done for the follower of Christ in the name of the Lord cannot fail of reward.

The Importance of Faithfulness and Integrity (Mark 9:42-50)

A fearful responsibility rests on those who profess to know Christ to do all they can to help rather than to hinder children. To cause one of the little ones who believe in Jesus to stumble is in His eyes a heinous offense. What a terrible thing it is to injure deliberately or mislead a little child—or, if one uses the term *little one* in a spiritual sense, a young convert. If one is tempted to injure them in any way let him keep in mind the solemn words of Mark 9:42-48.

If the hand would cause one to sin, let it be cut off, for "it is better...to enter into life maimed, than having two hands to go into hell"—that is, into Gehenna, the place of eternal judgment. "If thy foot offend thee, cut it off." If the feet would lead one into paths of sin, it would be far better to be footless and enter into life, than having two feet to be cast into the Gehenna of fire. Or if the eye would cause one to sin—and oh, how often sin enters through the eye—pluck it out. It is far better to enter into the kingdom of God with one eye than having two eyes to be cast into the Gehenna of fire.

Notice how the Lord reiterates the expression, "Where their worm dieth not, and the fire is not quenched." Though He was the tenderest and most gracious man who ever walked on this earth, He had more to say about the awfulness of eternal punishment for the finally unrepentant than anyone else whose teachings appear in the holy Scriptures. This description of Hell was possibly based on what was constantly visible at the lower part of the valley of the son of Hinnom, where all the refuse of the city was cast. In this valley perpetual fires were kept burning and there the carcasses of dead animals were thrown. Those passing by would see the gnawing worms and the unquenchable fire. It is an awful picture of the judgment that awaits the Christ-rejecter.

Some ancient manuscripts omit the latter part of verse 49, retaining only the words, "For every one shall be salted with fire." The thought is clear, however, even though the remainder of the verse might not rest on the best authority. "Every sacrifice shall be salted with salt." God had said concerning the sacrifices, "Neither shalt thou suffer the salt of the covenant of thy God to be lacking" (Leviticus 2:13). Salt preserves from corruption, and it would appear that the Lord is insisting here on that preservative power of righteousness which alone will deliver one from the judgment that sin so richly deserves.

Jesus had already spoken of His disciples as the salt of the earth, and in Mark 9:50 He adds, "Salt is good: but if the salt have lost his saltness, wherewith will ye season it?" Flavorless salt is utterly useless. And so a professed believer who is not characterized by righteousness has no testimony whatever for God. The Lord said, "Have salt in yourselves"— that is, let there be in your life and behavior that righteousness which glorifies God. Instead of seeking your own interest, seek the good of others, and thus "have peace one with another."

CHAPTER TEN

THE PATH OF DISCIPLESHIP

PART TWO

Jesus Answers Question on Divorce (Mark 10:1-12)

Passing down through Perea on the east of the Jordan, Jesus and His disciples came to the ford of Bethabara and crossed over into Judea. They were on the way to Jerusalem, where Christ was to fulfill His mission by dying as the great sin offering on a cross of shame. Although Jesus had been absent from Judea for some time, His fame preceded Him. Multitudes of the people resorted to Him. They were ready to hear what He had to say and according to His custom He took the opportunity to teach them.

Some of the sect of the Pharisees came to Him and questioned Him regarding divorce. They asked, "Is it lawful for a man to put away his wife?" The inquiry was not made sincerely. They were not looking for instruction, but rather for an opportunity to bring a formal accusation against Him. If possible they desired to expose Him as an unsafe and heretical teacher who taught contrary to the law of Moses.

He foiled them by asking them, "What did Moses command you?" They replied that Moses had permitted a bill of divorcement to be given and an unwanted or unloved wife to be put away. Jesus declared that this had been allowed because of the hardness of men's hearts, in order that a wife who had no favor in her husband's eyes might not have to endure even greater indignities than being divorced. But this was not God's highest thought as to the marriage relationship.

From the beginning when God made our first parents male and

female, He intended one woman to marry one man. "For this cause shall a man leave his father and mother, and cleave to his wife; and they twain [not they three, or more] shall be one flesh" (Mark 10:7-8). Therefore when two are united in wedlock they are no more to be considered as independent personalities free to go or stay as they please; they are one flesh.

Jesus added, "What therefore God hath joined together, let not man put asunder." Men may make laws that violate this divine order, but no human decree can nullify God's Word. Marriage is a life partnership. Elsewhere Jesus showed that if one of the contracting persons proves unfaithful and breaks the tie by cohabiting with another, the innocent one is free (Matthew 19:9). But apart from such a breach the tie is indissoluble save by death, as He made clear to His disciples when they were in the house again, away from the multitude. To divorce one's wife and marry another is to commit adultery. Likewise if a wife divorces her husband and marries another man, she becomes an adulteress.

Jesus Blesses the Children (Mark 10:13-16)

In these verses Jesus expressed His loving concern for little children. Parents who felt that the Lord would be interested in their little ones brought them to Him that He might lay His hands on them in blessing. Not understanding the heart of the Lord Jesus Christ, the disciples tried to restrain the parents, as though Jesus could not be troubled with children. They considered this an imposition, regarding it as below the dignity of their Master to be occupied with the little ones.

The Savior was displeased with the attitude of the disciples and He immediately revealed that He is the friend of children. He invited the parents to bring the children, assuring them that the little ones were typical members of the kingdom, because of their implicit faith in Him. Children are the ideal converts. When old enough to understand the story of the Lord Jesus, they are old enough to come to Him in trustful confidence. They enter into the kingdom of God when people considered older and wiser by human standards refuse to enter. When our Lord said of the little ones, "Of such is the kingdom of God," He was not implying that the children do not need to be regenerated in order to enter truly into that kingdom. They come from a lost race and are by nature children of wrath. But their simple faith makes them subjects of the kingdom, and in this they are examples to us all. Only as we manifest the same childlike faith do we enter into the kingdom of God.

"He took them up in his arms, put his hands upon them, and blessed them." Parents may be assured today that, though unseen by mortal eye, He takes our children in His loving arms and gives them His blessing as we bring them to Him in faith.

There are many today who, like the disciples, imagine that little children are too young to be brought to the Lord Jesus Christ. But His words are too clear to be misunderstood. He invites children to come to Him, and encourages parents to bring them. Elsewhere He speaks of "these little ones which believe in me" (Matthew 18:6), and He gives a solemn warning to any who put stumbling blocks before their inexperienced feet. We are right when we sing of Him, "There's a friend for little children." He is their friend, and He delights in their love and confidence and esteems them as His friends. It is a well-known fact that by far the greatest number of those who are now earnest Christians came to the Savior before they were twelve years of age.

Jesus Defines the Cost of Discipleship (Mark 10:17-31)

The incident with the rich young man has been appropriately designated, "the great refusal." Unlike many who questioned Jesus in order that they might trap Him in His words, this young man seems to have been, up to a point at least, intensely earnest. We are told that he came running and then, doing homage to Him, he fell upon his knees before Jesus as he inquired, "Good Master, what shall I do that I may inherit eternal life?"

Jesus took him up on his own legal ground. He first asked him why he used the term *good* in speaking to Him. Scripture says, "There is none that doeth good, no, not one" (Psalm 14:3). Why then address Jesus as good, unless indeed one recognized in Him the divine Son of God, for God alone is good? To this the young man made no reply.

Jesus then quoted the six commandments that summarize our responsibilities to our neighbors, including that which calls on us to honor our parents, who stand in the place of God to children in the home. The law said, "Keep my statutes . . . which if a man do, he shall live in them" (Leviticus 18:5).

Without a moment's hesitation the young man replied, "Master, all these have I observed from my youth." Outwardly he, like Saul of Tarsus before his conversion, was blameless concerning the righteousness of the law. What he did not realize was that all human righteousness is but as filthy rags in the sight of God, because of the corruption of the heart (Isaiah 64:6).

To test him and expose the hidden evil of his heart Jesus said, "One thing thou lackest: go thy way, sell whatsoever thou hast, and give to the poor, and thou shalt have treasure in heaven: and come, take up the cross, and follow me." It was a call to receive Christ as Savior and acknowledge Him as Lord. But he who seemed so earnest at first could not rise to the opportunity put before him. He professed to love his neighbor as himself but was not prepared to give up his wealth for the good of others. He was not ready to yield control of his life to Jesus. So he went away sorrowful, because his great wealth stood between him and allegiance to Christ. Did he ever repent? We do not know. So far as Holy Writ is concerned we know only that he went away in nature's darkness, because he turned from the light of life.

We can sense the pain in the heart of the Lord as He musingly said to His disciples, "How hardly shall they that have riches enter into the kingdom of God!" They were astonished to hear this, for undoubtedly they thought, as many do today, that poverty rather than wealth would be the greatest impediment to entrance into the kingdom. But Jesus explained the danger: putting one's trust in wealth can keep him from taking his rightful place before God as a needy sinner who can be saved only through grace. A camel could more readily pass through the eye of a needle than a rich man enter into the kingdom of God. Only those who judge themselves and come to God—only those who acknowledge their lost estate and spiritual poverty—find entrance there.

Amazed, the disciples asked, "Who then can be saved?" In reply Jesus told them that all things are possible with God. Even the rich may be brought to the place where they no longer trust in their wealth but in the living God.

The question naturally arises in our minds as to what prompted Peter to say, "Lo, we have left all, and have followed thee." Was he concerned as to the future of himself and his fellow disciples if the rich were not going to rally to the side of Jesus and assist Him in establishing the expected Messianic kingdom? Possibly so. His words seem to imply that he wondered whether they had risked all on a forlorn hope.

Jesus replied with words of assurance, though not at this time fully correcting His followers' carnal ideas of the coming kingdom. He gave the definite promise that no one would lose, but rather gain by sharing His path of rejection. But He warned them, "Many that are first shall be last; and the last first." That is, not everyone who gave promise of being a faithful and devoted follower would continue in the path of self-denial for Christ's name's sake, and some whose devotion seemed questionable, would prove genuine in the hour of trial.

To follow Christ means to share His cup of sorrow, to be misunderstood, and even hated and maligned by the world that lies in the hand of the wicked one. But the follower of Christ finds a joy, unknown to the world, in fellowship with the rejected King and in communion with fellow sufferers. He looks forward with assured hope to entering eternal life in the age to come. All believers now have eternal life abiding in them but in a decaying body. In the age to come we shall enter into life in all its fullness when the body as well as the soul is fully redeemed from the bondage of corruption.

Jesus Deals with Worldly Ambition (Mark 10:32-45)

As the little band moved on toward Jerusalem there was something in the bearing and appearance of Jesus that moved His disciples to fear and concern. In Luke 9:51 we read, "He stedfastly set his face to go to Jerusalem." He knew exactly what awaited Him there, and He went forward unflinchingly with a serious determination that evidently was expressed in His countenance, and caused the twelve to have a feeling of uneasiness. Were all their dreams of a coming glorious kingdom, in which He would declare Himself Messiah and deliver Israel from the Roman yoke, to be dissipated? Had they, after all, left everything they possessed and ventured all on a baseless hope?

Jesus sought to make them understand just what was before Him. He told them that when they reached Jerusalem the Son of man would be delivered to the religious leaders, who were ever His enemies and who would condemn Him to death. These leaders would turn Him over to their Gentile rulers who would mock and scourge Him, even spit in His blessed face, and finally put Him to death. But again He gave the promise, "The third day he shall rise again." But still they failed to comprehend His words, so obsessed were they with the thought that the kingdom should be set up immediately.

Giving evidence of how little they understood the mind of Christ, James and John said, "Master, we would that thou shouldest do for us whatsoever we shall desire." Their request was based on selfishness and worldly ambition, but the two brothers were doubtless unaware of the true condition of their hearts. The Lord Jesus desired to bring to the surface what was in their thoughts; so He pressed them to put the request in their own words.

"Grant...that we may sit, one on thy right hand, and the other on thy left hand, in thy glory." When James and John sought exalted positions in the coming kingdom, they showed how little they understood its true nature. They little realized how obnoxious to the Lord Jesus Christ were their ambitions. It is quite true that our Lord will bestow special honors on certain of His followers when He returns to set up His kingdom. He made this clear in several of His utterances (Matthew 19:28; Luke 19:17). But those who will occupy the highest places then will be those who were content to take the lowly places in the King's absence, and who were willing to suffer uncomplainingly for His sake.

"Ye know not what ye ask." The rebuke of the Lord Jesus was spoken not in anger but in love. Jesus wanted the disciples to learn the meaning of participation in His sufferings so they could share in the glories to follow. He wanted them to realize how little they understood what was about to take place. He asked them, "Can ye

drink of the cup that I drink of? and be baptized with the baptism that
I am baptized with?" He was referring to the cup of rejection and
judgment soon to be pressed to His lips, and to the baptism of death
He was to endure on the cross.

Not knowing what they said, James and John declared, "We can."
Their loyalty was evident, but the full nature of that cup and baptism
was hidden from them. Jesus replied that they would indeed drink of
His cup and be baptized with His baptism (for all who follow Him
have to taste the cup of rejection by the world and some are even
delivered unto death for His sake). However, Jesus went on to say
that no man can choose His own place in the kingdom that will be
displayed in power and glory. Each one will have the place for which
his life and service on earth have fitted him.

The other disciples also had desires for the highest offices, and
were indignant that John and James had forestalled them. It was very
difficult for the disciples to dissociate the thought of a kingdom from
dreams of positions of prominence for themselves. In the kingdoms
of the nations the great lord it over those of lesser degree. But in the
kingdom of God the very opposite rule prevails. The kingdom of
which Jesus Christ is Lord is a kingdom of love. There all are to seek
the blessing of others, and lowly service takes the place of haughty
authority. In the kingdom of Heaven those who labor for the blessing
of their fellows are recognized as great.

"Whosoever of you will be the chiefest, shall be servant of all."
Our Lord Himself is the pre-eminent example here. He who was
Lord of all became servant of all, that men might be brought to God.
We are called to follow in His steps. He left the glory of the Father's
side and came into this world. He became man in order that He might
die. Never once did He seek recognition from men. He was content
to be despised and rejected so that He might accomplish His great
mission of redemption. Dare we, who owe everything for eternity to
His humiliation, aspire to worldly honor and seek the approbation of
our fellow men rather than the approval of God?

Humility is one of the loveliest flowers that springs up in the
garden of the regenerated heart. We are all inclined to pride and
vanity by nature. When the Spirit of Christ possesses us, we exhibit
that lowliness and meekness which ever characterized our blessed

Lord. Where this lowly spirit prevails, it is easy to extend forgiveness to those who have offended us. To many this seems like slavish servility, but it is the very opposite. Greatness is evidenced by one's readiness to deny self and to serve others for Christ's sake, who "came not to be ministered unto, but to minister, and to give his life a ransom for many." We cannot share in His atoning or redemptive work, but we can and should follow Him in His life of patient service for the blessing of a needy world.

Jesus Heals Blind Bartimaeus (Mark 10:46-52)

To this poor sightless beggar the coming of the Lord Jesus was to mean the opening of his eyes, both physically and spiritually. He did not wait for Jesus to call him first, but "when he heard that it was Jesus of Nazareth, he began to cry out...Jesus, thou son of David, have mercy on me." Surely, such faith must have gratified the heart of the Lord.

Many of those who were in the crowd that followed Jesus as He passed through the city tried to silence Bartimaeus, but his faith refused to be deterred by their objection, and he continued to cry out. Assured in his soul that Jesus was the predicted Messiah, the offspring of David, Bartimaeus knew that Jesus could open his eyes if he could attract the Lord's attention. Faith like his never pleads in vain.

Jesus stopped and commanded the beggar to be called. It must have brought joy to the poor man's heart when they said, "Be of good comfort, rise; he calleth thee." Casting away his outer garment in his haste, he arose and came to Jesus. Doubtless he was guided by some kindly person in the crowd.

The Lord inquired tenderly, "What wilt thou that I should do unto thee?" Jesus knew well the desire of his heart, but He desired him to make a public confession of his need. "Lord," cried Bartimaeus, "that I might receive my sight."

His faith was at once rewarded. Jesus granted his request and gave him the additional assurance, "Thy faith hath made thee whole." In his exuberance and gratitude Bartimaeus followed Jesus as He went along the way. Though there is no evidence that he was called to give all his time to witnessing for Christ, what a testimony he had to give to the compassion and healing power of Him whom he had acclaimed as the Son of David!

CHAPTER ELEVEN
THE SERVANT IN JERUSALEM

The Triumphal Entry (Mark 11:1-11)

It is interesting and profitable to observe how the various outstanding events in our Lord's life were exactly predicted by prophets —divinely inspired men of God (2 Peter 1:21)—who lived hundreds of years before their words began to be fulfilled. Zechariah was one of the postexilic prophets who spoke of the sufferings of Christ and the glory that would follow (1 Peter 1:11; 5:1). In Zechariah 9:9 we see a graphic portrayal of Israel's rightful King entering His earthly capital: "Lowly, and riding upon an ass." But between the events described in this verse and those described in the verse immediately following, Jesus was to suffer a long period of rejection by His chosen people. Centuries were to roll by before the words of Zechariah 9:10 were to be fulfilled: "He shall speak peace unto the heathen: and his dominion shall be from sea even to sea, and from the river even to the ends of the earth." Yet all will come to fruition in God's appointed time.

The Holy Spirit alone could have foreseen the crucifixion of our Lord following so soon after what is often called the triumphal entry. Actually the nation of Israel did not officially acclaim Him as the promised King on that historic Palm Sunday. The leaders fiercely resented the homage paid Him and voiced their opposition in no uncertain terms. But to Jesus the welcome by the multitudes and the children (Matthew 21:15) was as a cup of cold water to His spirit after the bitter hatred He had experienced. He had given thanks before to the Father that "these things"—the mysteries of the kingdom—were hidden from the wise and prudent and revealed to babes (Matthew 11:25). This was confirmed in the reception accorded Him as He rode into the city of Jerusalem.

Mark 11 begins with an account of preparations for the triumphal entry. The last journey through Perea had been concluded, and Jesus and His disciples ascended the winding road from Jericho to Bethany on the slope of the mount of Olives. From there He prepared to enter the city where Jehovah had set His name. Jesus knew that the cross was just before Him, but for this purpose He had come into the world. It was nearing Passover in the spring of A.D. 30. He was about thirty-three years and six months of age—a comparatively young man, destined to be cut off in the middle of His life (Psalm 102:24).

The holy city is plainly visible from Olivet as one comes around the bend between Bethany and Bethphage. At this point Jesus waited until two disciples obtained the donkey on which He was to ride into Jerusalem in accordance with the prophetic word.

It made no difference to Jesus that the donkey brought to Him was an unbroken colt. He was the Creator come into this world as man, and as such all the lower creatures were subject to Him (Psalm 8:6-8). Only man, made in the image of God, rebelled against Him. All other creatures knew Him as their rightful owner (Isaiah 1:3).

If anyone questioned the disciples' right to loose the colt, they were to answer, "The Lord hath need of him." Evidently the owner of the beast knew Jesus and recognized His claims as pre-eminent.

The messengers had no difficulty finding the colt. All was as Jesus had said. The King James version says they found the colt "where two ways met." Many of the older commentators saw in this a picture of man himself, standing at the place of decision.

As Jesus had foreseen, some people questioned the right of the disciples to take the colt away. It is clear that these bystanders were not the owners, but simply observers who feared something wrong was being done. When explanation was given as the Lord had commanded, there was no further objection. Improvising a saddle with their flowing robes, the disciples prepared the colt to carry Jesus to the city.

"Hosanna; Blessed is he that cometh in the name of the Lord." In their holy enthusiasm the humble folk sought to give to the King a royal welcome. Divinely taught, they chanted the words of Psalm

118:26. They recognized the application of these words to the promised Messiah of Israel. *Hosanna* means "Save now" or "Deliver, we pray." It is the equivalent of "God save the king!" a customary cry in recognition of regal authority (2 Chronicles 23:11).

"The kingdom of our father David." For one brief moment Jesus was acknowledged as the rightful heir to the throne of David (Luke 1:32). But the time had not yet come for Him to ascend that throne. Not until He returns in glory will He build again the tabernacle of David that is thrown down (Acts 15:16; Amos 9:11-12).

Jesus entered the temple, as predicted in Malachi 3:1. Apparently He simply looked around the temple on this first day of His last week, although it is not easy to be certain as to this. The events recorded in Matthew 21:12-13 probably took place on His second visit to the city, as indicated in Mark 11:12,15.

As evening approached He went to Bethany with the disciples. In self-imposed banishment, He did not spend a night in the holy city during passion week. He recognized already that He was to suffer outside the gate (Hebrews 13:12-13). There was no place for Him in "the city of the great King" (Matthew 5:35). He found a refuge among the poor and the lowly and with those who waited for the consolation of Israel.

The Cleansing of the Temple (Mark 11:12-19)

On the day following the triumphal entry as Jesus and His disciples were going from Bethany to Jerusalem, Jesus was hungry. Having become man in all perfection He was subject to all the conditions under which sinful men live. A fig tree in full leaf by the wayside seemed to offer prospects of a feast of figs, but when Jesus went over to see it He found nothing but leaves, for the time of figs was not yet.

Jesus said, "No man eat fruit of thee hereafter for ever"—or, for the age. This fig tree was a type or symbol of Israel nationally, and its fruitless condition pictured the state of the nation—much religion but no fruit for God. So Israel remains barren and fruitless all through these centuries since Christ's rejection.

In Mark 11:15-17 we read of the second time Jesus cleansed the temple of those who were commercializing the holy things of the Lord. In John 2:13-16 we read of the first occasion, just shortly after He began His public ministry. But the merchants then reprimanded soon took advantage of His absence to reinstate their trade. No doubt in the beginning the sale of birds and beasts in the temple courts was intended simply as an accommodation for visitors who had come from distant lands to attend the annual feasts in Jerusalem. The same was true of the exchange of currency. Originally the money-changers were there to make it easy for these strangers to obtain the money that was used in Palestine in place of the coins of other lands. But what may have begun innocently enough had degenerated into a system of extortionate gains for those involved. Those of the dispersion who came to worship the God of their fathers were being systematically robbed of their savings—and all in the name of Jehovah!

Jesus dealt drastically with these covetous and dishonest merchants, overthrowing the tables of the money-changers, and driving out the sellers of doves and sacrificial lambs and other cattle. One can visualize Him as He stood before the amazed and frightened mob. His holy eyes were flashing with righteous indignation as He exclaimed, "Is it not written, My house shall be called of all nations the house of prayer? but ye have made it a den of thieves."

Naturally this aroused an unholy counter-indignation on the part of those who had upheld and profited by this commercializing of sacred things. These scribes and chief priests formed a cabal with the express purpose of seeking to lay hold of Jesus and to destroy Him. But they did not dare act openly as yet, because the people generally were stirred by the teaching and works of Jesus and inclined to think of Him as the promised Messiah. Therefore He was allowed to continue teaching that day in the temple courts. No one dared to interfere.

As evening came on He and His disciples left the city again, returning to the mount of Olives, possibly to Bethany.

A Lesson in Faith (Mark 11:20-26)

The next morning as they returned to Jerusalem they observed the barren fig tree now dried up from the roots. When Peter called attention to this, Jesus used the incident to emphasize the power of faith. Faith is trust or confidence. Such confidence should be in God, not in any human expedient. We can have faith in Him only as we rest upon His Word. In replying to his Sunday school teacher's inquiry, "What is faith?" the little boy was right in saying, "I think it is believing God and asking no questions."

When God speaks, we are to take Him at His Word. If therefore He made it clear that it was His will to remove a mountain from its established place and cast it into the sea, real faith could count on Him to act, and so would dare to command the mountain to disappear. Doubtless, behind the natural figure our Lord had in mind mountains of difficulty, such as Zerubbabel faced in Palestine when the returned remnant encountered such fierce opposition in the days of rebuilding the temple (Zechariah 4:7). Nothing is impossible with God, and he who is in fellowship with God can act in faith assured his request will be honored.

"Therefore I say unto you, What things soever ye desire, when ye pray, believe that ye receive them, and ye shall have them." Faith counts the things that are not as though they are. But we need to remember that these words apply only when we delight ourselves in the Lord, and so the desires of our hearts are according to His holy will (Psalm 37:4).

The state of the soul has much to do with the prayer of faith—hence the teaching on forgiveness given in Mark 11:25-26. God has never promised to answer the prayer of an unforgiving heart. An attitude of unforgiveness effectively blocks the channel of prayer so that no answer is possible. God forgives us as we forgive our brothers in Christ. This is not the forgiveness offered to a sinner, but to a failing saint. Unless we forgive others, our Father in Heaven will not forgive us when we come to Him acknowledging our sins from day to day.

This teaching as to prayer was given as the little company walked toward Jerusalem.

The Authority of Jesus (Mark 11:27-33)

When they entered Jerusalem, almost immediately Jesus was challenged by the irate scribes and chief priests concerning the cleansing of the temple. But He put them to silence by His answers.

The religious leaders questioned Him as to the source of His authority for cleansing the temple in the way He had done it. He refused to answer, but asked them instead, "The baptism of John, was it from heaven, or of men?" The right answer to His question would be the answer to their question. If they admitted that John was sent by God, then the claims of Jesus were established, for John had declared Him to be the promised One who was to baptize with the Holy Spirit and with fire—something that none but Messiah could do.

These cunning legalists debated among themselves as to how they should reply. If they admitted John was God's messenger to Israel they faced the inevitable question, "Why then did ye not believe him?" If they denied his divine commission they feared the people who firmly believed that John was a prophet. So they evaded the real question by answering, "We cannot tell." Jesus replied, "Neither do I tell you by what authority I do these things."

He was always ready to help honest inquirers. But these men were hypocritical objectors to His testimony. They were determined not to believe Him when His very works attested to His Messianic title and proclaimed Him to be that servant of Jehovah of whom Isaiah wrote, and for whom Israel had waited so long.

CHAPTER TWELVE
LESSONS OF THE SERVANT

Parable of the Vineyard (Mark 12:1-12)

This parable portrayed in a very vivid and graphic manner God's ways with Israel and their response and ingratitude throughout the past centuries. In the rejection and death of the heir we see the consummation of our Lord's ministry, to be followed by His glorious resurrection.

"The vineyard of the Lord of hosts is the house of Israel" (Isaiah 5:7). Settled by God in the land of Canaan, the Israelites had been cared for in a marvelous way. God had placed them under the care of those who should have watched for their souls and sought to cultivate them spiritually so that there would be abundant fruit for Him. But the husbandmen, or vine-dressers, thought only of their own selfish interests. They failed to render to Jehovah that love and reverence which He had the right to expect. When He sent His prophets to them they either "sent [them] away empty" (treated them with utter indifference) or else persecuted them even unto death for daring to reprove them because of their wickedness. Throughout the centuries this had been the attitude of the husbandmen. Now God had sent His Son as the final test of the love and loyalty of Israel. When the leaders saw Him they spurned His claim and sought His destruction. They said, "This is the heir; come, let us kill him, and the inheritance shall be ours."

Mark 12:8 is prophetic and was fulfilled just a few days later. "They took him, and killed him, and cast him out of the vineyard." It was thus that Jesus told them of His own rejection and death even before it came to pass.

Then He put the question to them: "What shall therefore the lord of the vineyard do?" The answer was plain: "He will come and destroy the husbandmen, and will give the vineyard unto others." Israel was to be set to one side while grace would flow out to the Gentiles.

This prophecy was in accord with what was written in Psalm 118:22: "The stone which the builders refused is become the head stone of the corner." So He spoke not only of death but of resurrection, because as the first begotten from the dead Jesus has been made the chief corner stone. "This was the Lord's doing, and it is marvellous in our eyes."

The parable and its application stirred the leaders to additional resentfulness. They realized He had spoken of them, but for the time being they dared not proceed against Him openly because they feared the reaction of the people generally.

Lesson on Paying Taxes (Mark 12:13-17)

The question of the tribute money was a live one throughout Palestine. To pay this tax was a tacit acknowledgment of Rome's authority, something that was thoroughly repugnant to Jews of strong nationalistic feeling. The Herodians and some others advocated this recognition of the imperial government because of special favor they hoped to get by their subservience.

It was not any desire to know the right or wrong of the matter that led the representatives of the two opposed schools of thought (the Pharisees and the Herodians) to put the question to Jesus, "Is it lawful to give tribute to Caesar, or not?" Despite their flattering way of addressing Him they were only setting a trap for Him. They hoped to ensnare Him into saying something that would give occasion either to accuse Him to their Roman overlords as an advocate of sedition, or to make it appear to the more intensely patriotic Jews that He had no sympathy with them in their yearning for deliverance from the Roman yoke.

"Why tempt ye me? bring me a penny [a denarius], that I may see it." His reply revealed that He saw into their hearts and knew exactly why they had come to Him.

When they handed one of the coins to Him, He inquired, "Whose is this image and superscription?" They replied, "Caesar's." He said to them, "Render to Caesar the things that are Caesar's, and to God the things that are God's." Thus they fell into the pitfall they had digged for His feet. They were amazed at His answer and were silenced so far as that subject was concerned.

Lesson on the Resurrection (Mark 12:18-27)

A group of Sadducees sought to entangle Jesus this time. They represented a materialistic sect that denied the resurrection and the existence of angels and spirits. Whether the story they put before Him was true or not we cannot say. It seems most unlikely, and may only have been an imaginary tale designed to cast ridicule on the doctrine of the resurrection.

According to the levirate order, if a man died leaving no heir his brother was to take the widow to be his own wife. The first child born of the new union would inherit the estate of the former husband. In the story the Sadducees told Jesus, this law was carried to an extreme. They said a certain woman had been wife to seven brothers in succession and had outlived them all. Seven brothers died one after the other and all were childless.

These cunning quibblers then presented what they evidently considered an unanswerable refutation of the resurrection of the dead. They asked, as recorded in Mark 12:23, "In the resurrection therefore, when they shall rise, whose wife shall she be of them? for the seven had her to wife."

Jesus was unperturbed, for He saw through their sophistry at once. He declared they were all in error for two reasons—their ignorance of the very Scripture which they professed to hold sacred, and their ignorance of the power of God. It was the Torah alone—that is, the books of Moses—that these Sadducees recognized as authoritative. So Jesus quoted from the book of Exodus in order to show the folly of their position.

The Sadducees denied the possibility of resurrection because they taught that the soul of man died with the body. Jesus explained that those who are physically dead are alive unto God, and that when the dead rise they do not again take up the same conditions that they knew on earth. They do not resume the marital state, but are as the angels in Heaven—sexless beings who do not have the power of reproducing their kind. The distinctions between man and woman will be done away in the resurrection. In the eternal condition following the rising from the dead, marriage will have no place. Each person will be a distinct individual capable of endless bliss or woe, but human relationships as we know them here will be ended.

Our Lord appealed to two great reasons for accepting the fact that the dead will rise. It is revealed in the Bible, which is God's inspired Word, and the resurrection rests on the power of the omnipotent God. When God has spoken, it is not for man to reason, but to accept His declaration with reverence. To ask how anything can be done because it is contrary to the ability of finite creatures is to forget that all power belongs to God, with whom nothing is impossible (Luke 18:27).

"God spake...saying, I am the God of Abraham, and...Isaac, and...Jacob." He did not say, "I was their God," but, "I am their God." He spoke of them as definite personalities related to Him by grace though their bodies had died long ago. In His own time they would rise again and be acknowledged as His own.

"He is not the God of the dead." If these patriarchs were reduced to unconsciousness or annihilated by death, He would not still be their God. But "all live unto him" (Luke 20:38). Though they are dead as to the body and hidden from the eyes of men, the God of the spirits of all flesh (Numbers 16:22) sees and knows everyone in his present state even when he is between death and resurrection. Jesus' answer was a crushing blow to the crass materialism of the Sadducees, and they found no words with which to make a reply.

The Scriptures teach not merely the survival of the soul after the body dies (Matthew 10:28). They also teach the literal physical resurrection unto life, or else a resurrection unto judgment (John 5:28-29). Resurrection is not reincarnation in some other form, as held by certain oriental mystics and their misguided occidental followers, but an actual rising from the dead of the very same person who died. Our Lord Himself came out of the grave in the same body that had hung on the cross. His resurrected body still bore the marks of His crucifixion (John 20:20,27). In like manner death will yield up the bodies of all men, even those that have long since been reduced to their chemical elements, for our God is the God of resurrection. He who created these bodies with all their marvelous powers can reassemble them when the time comes for the saved to be caught up to meet the Lord (1 Thessalonians 4:13-17). He can do the same later for the wicked when the time comes for them to rise and stand before the great white throne for judgment (Revelation 20:11-14). Surely nothing should have a more solemnizing effect on us as we remain in this world than the knowledge that this life is only a prelude for that which is to come. Life after death will last forever—either in the joy of Heaven or amid the sad and gloomy horrors of Hell. Faithfully Jesus Christ portrayed both aspects of the life beyond the grave, that none might presume or be deceived by the vain hope of a happy immortality if living and dying in sin. He would have all men remember that there are two resurrections, and following these, two destinies. Thus we learn the importance of receiving Christ now that we may be assured of joy hereafter.

Lesson on the Great Commandment (Mark 12:28-34)

The scribe who next came to question Jesus seems to have been an honest man of different character from the crafty hecklers who preceded him. He had been impressed by the sincerity of Jesus Christ and the clearness of His answers to the questions of others. He came inquiring, "Which is the first commandment of all?" He meant first in importance, not first in order.

"Jesus answered...The Lord our God is one Lord: and thou shalt love the Lord thy God with all thy heart, and with all thy soul, and with all thy mind, and with all thy strength." In these words from Deuteronomy 6:4-5 our Lord epitomized all the commandments that deal specifically with man's duty toward God. He who loves God supremely will not willingly dishonor Him in anything. The second commandment—"Thou shalt love thy neighbour as thyself"— was cited from Leviticus 19:18. It epitomizes all the precepts that have to do with man's duty toward other men. He who loves his neighbor will not desire to wrong him.

"Master, thou hast said the truth." The scribe was deeply impressed, and at once declared his sincere appreciation of the answer the Lord Jesus had given. He had affirmed the unity of the godhead. All Scripture-taught Jews held this as a cardinal truth. The scribe went on, "To love him...and to love his neighbour as himself, is more than all whole burnt offerings and sacrifices." The scribe showed real spiritual discernment. Nothing in the sacrificial ritual of the law was of any value in the sight of God if love were lacking. To love Him and to love one's neighbor wholeheartedly pleases God above all else.

"Thou art not far from the kingdom of God." With all his appreciation of the teaching of the Lord Jesus Christ, this scribe was not yet in the kingdom. He was, as it were, just outside the door. To step in he must receive Christ for himself—trust Him as Savior and own Him as Lord.

In the next instance it is Jesus Himself who asks the question and confounds His adversaries.

Lesson on Jesus' Identity (Mark 12:35-40)

It was a matter of common knowledge in Israel that the Messiah would be a son of David. God's promise to the psalmist-king was "There shall not fail thee (said he) a man on the throne of Israel" (1 Kings 2:4; Psalm 132:11). It is true that this promise depended on the seed of David walking in obedience to the Word of the Lord, but an unconditional promise had also been made, as set forth in Psalm 89:1-4,34-37. The teachers in Israel were right therefore in declaring that Christ—that is, Messiah (the Anointed)—was to be the Son of David. But they were ignoring other Scriptures that indicated He would also be the Son of God. So Jesus challenged them by drawing their attention to Psalm 110 and asking for an explanation. "How say the scribes that Christ is the son of David? For David himself said by the Holy Ghost, The Lord [Jehovah] said to my Lord [Adonai], Sit thou on my right hand, till I make thine enemies thy footstool."

Jesus proceeded to elucidate this passage by pointing out that it was the Messiah of whom David had spoken, and whom he acknowledged as his Lord. A divine person was to sit on the throne of the eternal—on the right hand of the Majesty on high. How then could such a one be David's son? We know the answer. They did not, and were afraid to attempt an explanation. Jesus is both son of David in His humanity, and Son of God in His divine nature. He was begotten in the womb of the virgin, without a human father. The whole mystery of the incarnation is wrapped up in this quotation from Psalm 110.

The common people were delighted by Christ's teaching and even seemed to enjoy the discomfiture of the scribes, whose manner of life was so contrary to their profession. Jesus warned the populace against the evil influence of these religious leaders. They loved to be conspicuous and to be lauded and admired for their apparent piety. Their garb marked them as a special class presumably worthy of recognition such as others did not merit. They appeared in long clothing and were pleased when they were the objects of the adulation of the common people. They loved the chief seats in the synagogues, and the best places at the feasts. The assumption was that these scribes were worthy of particular recognition because of their office, whatever their lives might be. Who can fail to see in all this the pretentiousness of clericalism?

The scribes were grasping and covetous, devouring widows' houses—that is, lending money on mortgage to needy widows and confiscating their property when they were unable to meet their obligations promptly. Yet all was done legally, so that the scribes would be above the charge of fraud. They covered their extortionate behavior and maintained an appearance of great piety by making long prayers in public places.

But a reckoning day is coming when all the secret things of the heart will be brought to light. Hypocrites such as these will receive just retribution.

Lesson on Giving (Mark 12:41-44)

Following the denunciation of those who obtained riches unjustly, Jesus took occasion to commend the generosity of a poor widow, who may have been one of those despoiled by the scribes.

"Jesus sat over against the treasury." He does this still. He takes note of all that is given for the maintenance of the testimony of God and the relief of human wretchedness. It is evident that a box for contributions was placed at or near one of the entrances to the temple courts. There the faithful might put their gifts for the upkeep of the worship and service of the Lord. The poor widow came and threw in "two mites, which make a farthing," possibly all she had earned that day by hard work in the service of some rich family. Jesus looked on and observed "how the people cast money into the treasury." He took note of the amounts put in and the manner in which this was done. Doubtless many gave very ostentatiously, anxious that others should give them credit for great generosity.

Heaven's method of computing values is altogether different from earth's method. We are accustomed to judge by the amount given. The Lord estimates the value of the gift by the amount one has left! So Jesus testified, "I say unto you, That this poor widow hath cast more in, than all they which have cast into the treasury." He proceeded to show how He arrived at so amazing a conclusion. The rich had given out of their abundance. After making their contributions they had vast sums left to use as they chose. But the widow had held back nothing. She had cast in all her living—that is, all her earnings for the entire day. Such is Heaven's way of recognizing gifts for the work of the Lord.

CHAPTER THIRTEEN
REVELATIONS OF THE FUTURE

Introduction

Mark 13 should be read and studied carefully in connection with Matthew 24 and Luke 21. All three chapters give us a report of our Lord's Olivet discourse, in which He traced prophetically the conditions that were to prevail in Palestine and among the Gentile nations after His rejection and resurrection. His prophecies included the destruction of Jerusalem under Titus and—going on to the climax—the second coming of the Son of man and the establishment of the kingdom of God on earth in power and glory. It is noteworthy that when He spoke in His servant character as the prophet of Jehovah, He declared His self-limitation: "Of that day and that hour knoweth no man, no, not the angels which are in heaven, neither the Son, but the Father" (Mark 13:32). As the perfect Servant He chose not to know what the Father was not pleased to reveal (Deuteronomy 18:15,18-19).

We do not find in these three chapters any mention of the church of the present dispensation. When Jesus spoke these words, the truth as to the body of Christ was still unrevealed. This mystery was not made known until it was given by special illumination to the apostle Paul and through him to others some time after the present age of grace began. Therefore in reading the Olivet discourse we do well to recognize its strictly Jewish character. While the discourse reveals much hitherto kept secret, there is no intimation in it of the origin, course, or destiny of the church—the heavenly people now linked by the Spirit with the risen Christ.

Many of those who heard this address were incorporated into the church of the present dispensation by the baptism in the Holy Spirit on Pentecost and after. Yet all who heard are viewed as the Jewish remnant waiting for the consummation of the Old Testament prophecy—the setting up of Messiah's kingdom when the once-rejected Servant of Jehovah will return to rule the nations with the iron rod of inflexible righteousness (Psalm 2). The elect in view throughout the discourse of Mark 13 are therefore the early saints—both Jews and converted Gentiles in the last days (the seventieth week of Daniel 9)—who are to be gathered from all parts of the world to welcome the King when He sets up His throne on mount Zion. If these considerations be kept in mind much confusion will be avoided.

Characteristics of the Present Age (Mark 13:1-8)

Jesus and His followers left the city on the evening of the day in which He had been in controversy with the unbelieving leaders regarding several definite questions. As they left Jerusalem the disciples took pardonable pride as Jews in calling His attention to the magnificent buildings of the temple and nearby palaces. Doubtless they thought that Jesus would soon take these over, and they would dwell in them with Him and help Him administer the affairs of the kingdom. But to their amazement He declared that of all those great buildings not one stone would be left upon another, but all would be razed.

Pausing, Jesus sat on the mount overlooking the temple, and four of the disciples—Peter, James, John, and Andrew—asked Him privately, "Tell us, when shall these things be? and what shall be the sign when all these things shall be fulfilled?"

In Mark 13:5-8 the Lord outlined the course of the present age and speaks of the general characteristics that will prevail during the time of His physical absence from the world. There will be no improvement in morals or in the affairs of nations. The Prince of Peace has been rejected. Consequently there can be no lasting peace until He returns to reign and put down all unrighteousness.

Many false christs were predicted and the predictions have been abundantly fulfilled, but the true sheep of the flock have not been deceived by the voices of these strangers. There will be wars and rumors of wars because the only One who could have saved the nations from these calamities has been spurned and crucified. Jesus clearly foresaw all this and therefore pictured exactly the age following His rejection by the world and His ascension to Heaven.

Ever since He left this earth, that which is outlined in verse 8 has been exemplified. Nation has risen against nation, and kingdom against kingdom. Great disturbances have filled men's hearts with dread, while famines and other troubles have made this world a scene of sadness and distress. Yet these things are but the beginning of sorrows, even though they have continued for nearly twenty centuries. The worst of all suffering is yet in the future.

Far worse are the dangers to which men are to be subjected in the time of the end, when God's final judgments are falling on the earth. But even then—in the time of Jacob's trouble and the era of trial that is to come on all those who dwell in the world—the message of the gospel will be proclaimed until the final consummation of the age.

Signs of the Last Days (Mark 13:9-13)

We of this present age may appropriate the words of Mark 13:9-13 to ourselves when we are in similar circumstances, but it is important to see their exact application. The suffering saints referred to here are clearly those of Israel who will be God's final witnesses after the church as we know it has been caught away to Heaven and the last week of Daniel 9 has begun. Then God will raise up a host of wise ones (the Maskilim of Daniel 12) to bear testimony and proclaim the gospel of the kingdom among all nations. These saints will be the special objects of Satan's enmity and will be exposed to fearful suffering and relentless persecution. Nevertheless the gospel must be proclaimed to all nations before the end will come.

While portraying this time of persecution, Mark 13:11-13 also gives comfort and encouragement to those who will suffer arrest and imprisonment in those dark days. The Holy Spirit of God will enable them to answer those who accuse them falsely. The saints will be enabled to answer in a manner that their adversaries will not be able to resist. This passage might seem to apply only to this present dispensation of grace when the Holy Spirit indwells all believers. But we need to remember that even when His present work in the church comes to an end and He no longer personally indwells the saints, He will still be omnipresent. He will be with all who turn to Christ in those dark days, even as He was with Old Testament saints before Pentecost.

Betrayal by one's own relatives, even unfilial children giving evidence against godly parents, will call for great patience on the part of those who will be witnesses to the coming King in that time of stress. Those who confess Christ as earth's rightful King will be tried to the utmost. They will be hated by all who are subject to the power of Satan working through the atheistic governments of the last days. "But he that shall endure unto the end, the same shall be saved." This is not to say that salvation in that hour of crisis will depend on individual faithfulness, but rather that endurance to the end is the evidence of reality. Mere profession will break down then, as now. But if one has actually been regenerated, no matter what he may be called on to endure, he will be given power to continue in the path of devotedness to the Lord.

The Great Tribulation and Christ's Second Coming (Mark 13:14-27)

It is clear from the ninth chapter of Daniel that the last week will be divided into two parts. The entire period is called a "time of trouble" (Daniel 12:1), and "the time of Jacob's trouble" (Jeremiah 30:7). But it is the last part—the three and a half years beginning with the full revelation of the man of sin—that is designated "the great tribulation." This will be ushered in by the setting up of the abomination of desolation predicted in Daniel 12:11.

We need to distinguish between "the abomination that maketh desolate" spoken of in Daniel 11:31, which refers to the image of Jupiter set up in the temple by Antiochus Epiphanes in the distant past, and the "abomination that maketh desolate" of Daniel 12:11, which refers to a desecration yet to take place. It is this latter abomination of which our Lord was speaking. Whether the abomination will be a literal image of the beast (Revelation 13:14-15) to be erected by the false prophet, the lamb-like beast (the antichrist) of the last days, or a symbol of some secret agency acting on behalf of the blasphemous head of the coming world empire, we may not be positive. But in the light of the Lord's words the remnant living in that hour of trial will understand. They will also know that the power of evil can last only 1260 days thereafter, and at the end of that time the kingdom will be set up. The great tribulation therefore will go on throughout three and a half years after this abomination is revealed. This will be the time when the wrath of God will be poured out on apostate Christendom and apostate Judaism. To Christians the promise is given that they will not be exposed to wrath. We look for our Lord Jesus to snatch us away from the wrath to come (1 Thessalonians 1:10).

The instructions given in Mark 13.14-18 apply particularly to the Jewish remnant in Palestine during the reign of the beast and the antichrist. As in the days of Titus, warning is given to the remnant to avoid the city and to flee to the wilderness where they will be protected from the wrath of the devil expressed through the antichrist.

Daniel predicted "a time of trouble, such as never was since there was a nation even to that same time" (Daniel 12:1). In Mark 13:19 Jesus used similar language. So terrible will be the catastrophe that will fall on the nations that except the Lord shorten the days "no flesh should be saved." But He told us that for the elect's sake—referring to the elect of Israel and those who will be spared out of the nations—those days will be shortened.

Three and one-half years equals approximately 1278 days. But the power of the beast will be limited to 1260 days. The period will be shortened by 18 days to permit the salvation of many from actual destruction.

In that awful time of strong delusion and hardness of heart many will be misled by false christs and false prophets, as well as by the supreme antichrist at Jerusalem. But the elect of God will be preserved from the deceivers' blinding influence. To the elect Jesus said, "Take ye heed: behold, I have foretold you all things."

Observe that all the portents described in Mark 13:24-25 and the actual return of the Son of man are to take place immediately "after that tribulation" and therefore have not yet taken place. It is certain that the prophecy of the great tribulation (Mark 13:14-23) does not refer to any event already fulfilled—for instance, the destruction of Jerusalem or persecutions of the church under either pagan or papal Rome—for the Lord's second advent is still in the future. How near it may be none but God can say; but it is still the expectation of the people of God, and not something to which they can look back.

Christ's coming to the earth will be attended with great natural convulsions. Everything that can be shaken will reel to and fro like a drunken man and supernatural events will occur among the heavenly bodies. In this nuclear age we can readily see how literally these words of Jesus can be taken.

Note the difference between this stage of the second advent and that depicted in 1 Thessalonians 4. In Mark 13 the Son of man comes to the earth with power and great glory. In 1 Thessalonians 4 the Lord descends from Heaven, but calls His saints to meet Him in the air. In Mark 13 He sends forth His angels to gather His elect (the remnant out of Israel and the nations waiting for His return) from the four winds, from the uttermost part of the earth to the uttermost part of Heaven. In 1 Thessalonians 4 the saints of the past ages and of the church, the body of Christ, will be raptured (caught up) to meet Him in the air in order to return with Him in glory when the passage in Mark 13 is fulfilled.

Our Duty to Watch (Mark 13:28-37)

In this section of Mark 13 the fig tree is used as a symbol of Judah, or the Jewish people. It speaks of Israel nationally. When the fig tree puts forth her leaves one may know that summer is near. "So...when ye shall see these things come to pass"—that is, when the Jews once more acquire national consciousness and the predicted signs begin to come to pass—you will know that the consummation (the coming of the King) is at hand. Until that day the unbelieving Jews will abide. All Satan's efforts will be unable to destroy them. No matter how unbelievers may scoff, God's Word will stand. Heaven and earth may pass away, but His words will never pass away.

It is useless to try to work out some chronological system to determine the time of His coming. This is a secret, unrevealed even to angels. Even the Son, as man on earth, chose not to know. It is the

Father's prerogative to set the time, as Jesus also declared in Acts 1:7. How slow men have been to accept this, and what blunders they have made by attempting to compute the time of His return.

Like a man gone on a journey who gave instruction to his servants as to their duties in his absence but did not intimate the day or hour of his return, so Jesus our Lord has ascended to Heaven. He declared that in due time He will come again but He did not name the time. Meanwhile we are here to serve Him. He has appointed "to every man his work, and commanded the porter to watch." It is for us to take heed to His words, to watch and pray, as we wait for the fulfillment of His promise. Because of the uncertainty of the hour when He will come back to earth all His servants should ever be on the *qui vive*, waiting and watching expectantly lest coming suddenly He find them sleeping. To every one the word is spoken—"Watch."

CHAPTER FOURTEEN
THE SUPREME SACRIFICE

PART ONE

Mary's Devotion (Mark 14:1-9)

Events now moved on rapidly to the consummation, when our blessed Lord was to die on the cross as the great sin-offering. In the Gospel of Matthew Jesus is seen as the trespass offering, restoring that which He took not away (Psalm 69:4). In Mark's account we see Jesus giving up His life to meet all God's claims against sin. Sin here is viewed not only as actual trespass, but also as that which is innate in the heart of fallen man who displays his hostility to God in acts of rebellion. The steps leading directly to the cross are all intensely solemn and deeply instructive.

We note the ever-increasing enmity of the chief priests and scribes in Mark 14:1-2. These wily hypocrites were too crafty to risk arresting Jesus openly on the feast day. There would be too many of the common people in Jerusalem at that time. So they plotted secretly, waiting for a propitious hour in which to carry out their nefarious plans.

Meantime a little group of those who loved Jesus sought to honor Him in a special way. The home at Bethany, where Mary, Martha, and Lazarus lived was for our blessed Lord one of the brightest spots on earth. It was one place where He was always welcome and where His mission was understood to a large extent. Mary perhaps comprehended His thoughts better than the others, for she learned at His feet what may have been hidden from her busier sister and even from Lazarus himself. To these three the Lord Jesus could allow His affection to go out in a way He could not always allow it to go out to others. We read that Jesus "loved Martha, and her sister, and Lazarus" (John 11:5), and it is very evident that they appreciated and reciprocated that affection. When Lazarus was ill, the sisters thought it was quite sufficient to send a messenger to Jesus to say to Him, "He whom thou lovest is sick" (John 11: 3).

It is interesting to note how the Holy Spirit speaks of Bethany as "the town of Mary and...Martha" (John 11:1). Doubtless many important people lived in that suburban city so near to Jerusalem, and one might have identified Bethany more naturally with them than with this quiet unassuming family. But to God it was *their* town, because they loved and believed in His Son. Is not this the way the Lord looks on our cities and villages today? He values them not as the places of residence of those who are great in the eyes of the world, but rather as the dwelling places of some of His saints—the "quiet in the land" (Psalm 35:20); the poor of this world, rich in faith (James 2:5); those unknown to men, yet well known to God (2 Corinthians 6:9).

We know nothing about Simon the leper, but the presumption is that he had been a leper and had been cleansed by Jesus. Some have supposed he was the husband of Martha; others that he was father of the three who were such intimate friends of Jesus.

I know that some take it for granted that there are two different women involved in the varying accounts of the anointing of the Lord in Bethany (see Matthew 26:6-13 and John 12:2-8). But this idea seems utterly preposterous in view of the fact that practically the same conversation is given in each account. In each instance the disciples object to the waste of the ointment, on the ground that it might have been sold for three hundred pence and the money given to the poor. In each case the Lord defends the woman for what seemed to them like waste and expresses His personal appreciation of her action. To me His words prove conclusively that it was Mary of Bethany—the sister of Martha and Lazarus—who anointed the Lord, and only she. She considered nothing too precious for Jesus upon whose head and feet also (as John tells) she poured the spikenard as He reclined at the table. Her anointing of Jesus was a beautiful tribute to the One whom she recognized as the promised Messiah.

"Why was this waste of the ointment made?" asked some. Judas, we know from John's account, was the prime spirit in this murmur of discontent. It indicated how little he and the rest understood of the events soon to take place, though Jesus had foretold them again and again. Mary anointed His body beforehand for its burial (Mark 14:8).

"It might have been sold for...three hundred pence, and have been given to the poor." The Roman penny (denarius) was a silver coin of a little less value than our twenty-five cent piece, but the penny had far greater purchasing power and was the ordinary daily wage of a laboring man in those times. According to the computation of Judas, the ointment represented a full year's wages if the sabbath and special feast days were omitted. This amount seemed too much to lavish on Jesus, but true love knows no limit on what it delights to give and do for the beloved. The suggestion that the money might rather have been used in almsgiving did not mean that Judas cared for the poor. We are told he objected "because he was a thief, and had the bag, and bare away what was put therein" (John 12:6, literal rendering).

Jesus always appreciated every evidence of sincere affection and He placed a high value on Mary's act of devotion. Nothing is wasted that is lavished on Jesus our Lord. He deserves the best we have. He gave all for us. Mary's act of worship was an apt illustration of what we read in Song of Solomon 1:12. She recognized in Jesus Israel's true King.

"Ye have the poor with you always...me ye have not always." It is ever right and proper to minister to the needy, who can always be found if we desire to help them. Such ministry is commendable at all times. But Jesus was about to leave this world, and Mary seemed to realize this.

"She hath done what she could." There can be no higher commendation than this. All cannot do great things for Christ, but each one should do what he can as unto the Lord Himself. Mary had no thought that day that her kindly expression of love for the rejected King was to make her name known throughout the entire world. Her story is told in three of the Gospels and has been carried throughout every land where Christ is preached.

These three friends of Jesus illustrate three qualities that should characterize all believers in Him. In Martha we see service, which is at its best when free from worry and anxiety and done as unto the Lord Himself. In Mary we see discipleship and worship. She delighted to take the place of a learner at the feet of Jesus and to pour out her choicest treasure upon Him. Lazarus, who dined with Him (John 12:2), speaks of communion or fellowship. Blessed it is when all these characteristics are seen in any one individual!

The Last Passover (Mark 14:10-21)

Judas Iscariot was apparently the only one of the twelve who was not a Galilean. *Iscariot (Ish-Kerioth)* means a "man of Kerioth," a city of Judah. As treasurer of the apostolic company (John 12:6) he was trusted by the rest, but all the time he was unrenewed in heart and life (John 6:70). Professing to be a son of God (Acts 1:17) he was really "the son of perdition" (John 17:12), destined because of his own sins to a lost eternity in endless woe. This was "his own place" (Acts 1:25). Though so highly privileged, it would have been better for him had he never been born (Matthew 26:24).

The Pharisees promised to pay him for the betrayal of Jesus. Covetousness, the love of money, is a root from which every form of evil may spring (1 Timothy 6:10). Covetousness led Judas to betray his Master to those who sought His death.

Simeon said of the Lord Jesus Christ, when he took the holy baby in his arms at the presentation in the temple, that through Him the thoughts of many hearts would be revealed (Luke 2:35). Jesus Christ is the touchstone of all hearts. Everything depends on our attitude toward Him. Judas, who accompanied Him for some three years, basely betrayed Him. Peter, true in heart yet filled with the spirit of cowardice, denied any connection with Him. Pilate, convinced of His innocence, weakly gave in to those who clamored for His death and sentenced Him to the cross. These three representative men set forth the various ways in which people still act toward the Christ of God.

When the day came that the Passover lamb was to be sacrificed, the disciples inquired as to where they should keep the feast with their Master. As visitors in Jerusalem they had no home of their own in which to observe this sacred rite. But it was customary for many households to provide a guest room that strangers in Jerusalem might use freely in order to carry out the directions given in the law regarding the Passover.

Jesus had foreseen the need for a room. He sent two of His disciples into the city with specific instructions to look for a man carrying a pitcher of water. It was the women who ordinarily carried the water in earthenware pitchers or ewers on their heads or shoulders, so a man carrying water would be easily identified. When the man met the disciples, they were to follow him into whatever house he entered and were to say to the host of that home, "The Master saith, Where is the guestchamber, where I shall eat the passover with my disciples?" The host would immediately show them a large furnished upper room in which they were to arrange the paschal meal. Following the instructions given, the two disciples went into the city and found everything exactly as Jesus had said and they prepared the Passover feast.

In the evening, which was the beginning of the fourteenth of Nisan (the same day on which Jesus was to die as the antitypical paschal lamb), He came with His twelve disciples, including the traitor Judas. They sat or reclined at the table on which were placed the various dishes that were appointed in the law, and the cups of wine that had become customary.

As they observed the feast in solemn silence Jesus spoke saying, "Verily I say unto you, One of you which eateth with me shall betray me." Startled by what seemed incredible, the eleven questioned Him with honest hearts asking, "Is it I?" Judas hypocritically made the same inquiry. Jesus replied, "It is one of the twelve, that dippeth with me in the dish." Then He added "The Son of man indeed goeth, as it is written of him: but woe to that man by whom the Son of man is betrayed! good were it for that man if he had never been born." One might think that statement would have touched the hardest heart.

What were the feelings of Judas as he heard these words? We are not told and it is useless to speculate. But a little later when Jesus turned to Judas and said, "That thou doest, do quickly," he arose and went out immediately into the night (John 13:27).

The Lord's Supper (Mark 14:22-31)

The Passover feast, the annual memorial of Israel's deliverance from Egyptian bondage, was about to close when Jesus inaugurated another feast. It became the memorial of His death and the redemption accomplished thereby. (Apparently the Lord's supper was instituted after the exit of Judas.)

Jesus took one of the flat unleavened Passover loaves and after giving thanks broke it and gave it to the disciples. He said, "Take, eat: this is my body." Certainly no one there dreamed for one moment that Jesus meant that the bread was transubstantiated into His actual flesh. While they could not know all that was involved in that simple act, they at least knew that He meant the bread symbolized His body.

Later Jesus took the cup which held the fruit of the vine, the blood of the grape. After giving thanks for this also, He passed the cup to the eleven and they all drank of it. He explained, "This is my blood of the new testament, which is shed for many." And He added, "Verily I say unto you, I will drink no more of the fruit of the vine, until that day that I drink it new in the kingdom of God." They could not understand the meaning of His words at the time, but later all would be made plain.

The Greek word rendered "testament" in the King James version is also translated "covenant." The disciples knew God had promised to make a new covenant with Israel and Judah—a covenant of pure grace. The first covenant at Sinai was confirmed by the sprinkling of blood. The cup of which the disciples partook spoke of the blood whereby the new covenant was to be sealed.

"When they had sung an hymn." This was, in all probability, what was known then as "the little hallel," consisting of Psalms 113–118. Think of Jesus, with the cross so near and to Him so visible, leading the praises of the little company! When the memorial feast had ended, they left the upper room and wended their way to Gethsemane.

As they moved slowly along the way from the house in which they had eaten the Passover, out through the gate of the city, and across the viaduct to the mount of Olives, Jesus warned the disciples of their coming defection. He, the Shepherd, was to be smitten, as Zechariah had prophesied. They, the sheep of His flock, were all to be scattered

(Zechariah 13:7). But He gave again the promise of resurrection, and He reminded them that He would then go before them to meet them in Galilee.

Self-confident and knowing not his own weakness, Peter declared, "Although all shall be offended [or stumbled], yet will not I." Jesus told him that before the cock would crow twice he would three times deny any knowledge of the One he had owned as Master. In the other Gospels it is reported that He said, "Before the cock crow." There is no contradiction. Cock-crowing was a definite time—three o'clock in the morning. In Mark 14:30 we learn that Jesus also indicated the crowing twice of a specific cock.

Unimpressed, Peter vociferated, "If I should die with thee, I will not deny thee in any wise." The other ten made the same affirmation.

The Garden of Gethsemane (Mark 14:32-52)

At last Jesus and the disciples reached Gethsemane, the garden where He had often gone to pray and commune with His Father. He left eight of the disciples near the entrance and asked them to sit there while He went on to pray. He took Peter, James, and John with Him into the garden, and they saw a great change come over Him. His usual calm gave place to agitation of spirit. They realized He was entering some great crisis, but they could not understand even when He declared, "My soul is exceeding sorrowful unto death." Jesus asked the three to wait there and watch while He went farther into the depths of the olive grove.

In anticipation of drinking the cup of wrath that our sins had filled, Jesus prayed in agony that, if it were possible, the hour and the cup might pass from Him. His holy soul shrank from the awfulness of being made sin. It was not death but the divine anger against sin—the imputation of all our iniquities to Him—that filled His soul with horror. There was no conflict of wills. He was in all things submissive as He prayed, "Abba, Father, all things are possible unto thee; take away this cup from me: nevertheless not what I will, but what thou wilt."

In this supreme test of His subjection to the Father's will, Jesus proved Himself to be the obedient Son who always did those things that pleased His Father. But He could not have been the holy Man He was if He could have contemplated the cross and the bitter cup of judgment against sin with equanimity. The holier one is the more he suffers from imputation of sin.

Returning to the three disciples He found them sleeping. Addressing Peter who had made such protestations of loyalty, He gently reproved him: "Couldest not thou watch one hour?" Then He implored them all to watch and pray lest they enter into temptation, for while their spirits were willing, their flesh was weak.

Once more Jesus went on into the darkness and prayed as before. He returned the second time and found the three asleep again. He prayed a third time and came again to them. His agony having passed, He looked sorrowfully on the disciples and said, "Sleep on now, and take your rest." Then He added, "It is enough, the hour is come; behold, the Son of man is betrayed into the hands of sinners." He then bade them rise up, as the betrayer was at hand.

Already a multitude led by Judas were making their way through the garden to the trysting place that he knew so well. He told them that he would identify the One they sought by greeting Him with a kiss. As he came to where Jesus was waiting quietly, Judas stepped up to Him and said, "Master, master"—that is, "Rabbi, Rabbi." Judas kissed Him repeatedly, as the original implies.

The soldiers laid hands on Jesus and bound Him in order to lead Him away. At the sight of his Master thus betrayed and ill-treated, Peter's spirit was stirred and he began slashing about with his sword. But all he accomplished was to slice off the ear of Malchus, a servant of the high priest—an act that might have cost Peter his life later. However, we learn in Luke 22:51 that Jesus put forth His hand and healed the wounded man.

Turning to the armed rabble He inquired, "Are ye come out, as against a thief, with swords and with staves [or rods] to take me?" Jesus reminded them that He had taught openly in the temple. Why had they not arrested Him on one of those occasions? But all was permitted by God that the prophetic Scriptures might be fulfilled.

Realizing something of the seriousness of the situation, all the disciples fled panic-stricken, leaving Jesus alone with His captors.

There was one unnamed youth who followed Jesus closely. The

youth was dressed only in a linen cloth wound around his body. Some in the company of the captors sought to lay hold on him also, but he too fled, leaving the cloth in their hands and disappearing naked among the trees of the garden. Who was this young man? Was it John Mark himself, the author of this Gospel? Many have thought so because of the fact that he alone mentioned the incident, and did so without identifying the youth. We will never know for certain until we stand at the judgment seat of Christ.

The infamous behavior of Judas in betraying Jesus to the leaders of Israel fills us with indignation. We are angry when we realize that one so favored could behave so abominably, but his behavior was simply the exemplification of what is in all our hearts if unrestrained by divine grace. Jesus endured the betrayal with quiet dignity and with no evidence of anger or ill-will toward the one who was treating Him so wickedly.

Jesus' Accusers (Mark 14:53-65)

The first terror over, at least two of the disciples—John and Peter—returned and followed the crowd to the house of the high priest where Jesus was to have His first hearing, if such it could be called. Mark did not tell of John, who was related to the house of Caiaphas and who ventured boldly inside the house (John 18:15-16). But Peter followed at a distance until all were either inside the palace proper or in the porch.

The arrest of the Lord Jesus Christ in the night and His being dragged to the court of the high priest before dawn was illegal. But the Jewish leaders, ordinarily so punctilious about obeying the traditions of the elders, forgot all such details in their desire to get rid of Jesus Christ.

"Peter followed him afar off...and he sat with the servants." Peter's declension began months before when he dared to rebuke the Lord Jesus (Matthew 16:22). He may have become exalted because of the very gracious commendation of Jesus a little earlier (Matthew 16:17-19). From that time on we see one evidence of failure after another. Now he who had boasted that he would never forsake his Lord followed at a distance and sat in the company of the ungodly.

Yet it was love for his Lord that drew him back and led him to follow, though afar off, that he might see the end of the affair that was so contrary to all his hopes and expectations.

In vain the leaders looked for proof of any perfidy on the part of Jesus. Although they had suborned conscienceless false witnesses to accuse Him, their testimony was so contradictory that it could not be used to discredit Him. Finally Caiaphas challenged Jesus as to why He did not reply or seek to clear Himself of these false accusations, but there was no answer.

Nonplused but determined to find some reason to convict the prisoner, the high priest inquired, "Art thou the Christ, the Son of the Blessed?" Jesus replied with perfect calmness, "I am: and ye shall see the Son of man sitting on the right hand of power, and coming in the clouds of heaven." This answer implied that He was the Son of man spoken of in Daniel 7 who was to receive the kingdom from the Ancient of Days.

Filled with indignation and appearing to be horror-stricken, Caiaphas forgot the law that forbade a high priest to rend his garments, and he tore his robe. He declared that there was no need for any further witnesses, for all had heard the blasphemy uttered by the lips of Jesus. What did such a One deserve? Unanimously they condemned Him to death.

Then ensued a shameful scene that would have disgraced any court, were the prisoner ever so guilty. Some spat on His sacred countenance. Others blindfolded Him, and as they slapped Him insultingly they cried derisively, "Prophesy," asking that He name those who were so mistreating Him. But no word came from His holy lips.

The betrayal, mock trial, and condemnation to death of our blessed Lord form together the most colossal miscarriage of justice in all history. Yet everything was foreseen by God and all was in accord with the sure word of prophecy. Little though they realized it, those who participated in this infamous crime were playing parts long since predicted. It is not that they were foreordained to act as they did. They were free moral agents in one sense because they acted deliberately according to their own wills. But they were slaves of Satan, the great archenemy of God and man, who led them on to do what God Himself had declared would be done. There is a difference between His foreknowledge and His foreordination—a difference that Peter made clear at Pentecost when he declared, "Him, being delivered by the determinate counsel and foreknowledge of God, ye have taken, and by wicked hands have crucified and slain" (Acts 2:23). Every adverse actor in that most awful drama of the ages was individually responsible for his behavior toward the holy Savior, even though it was by means of their actions that He was brought to the cross where He offered up Himself as a propitiation for our sins.

Peter's Denial (Mark 14:66-72)

As Jesus was being disgraced, Peter met his great test and failed as he had been forewarned only a few hours before. "Peter was beneath in the palace." His rightful place would have been in the company with his Lord, but fear kept him from openly identifying himself with the Savior in this hour of testing.

One of the maidservants accused him of following Jesus. Evidently she had seen him in the company of the Lord Jesus on some other occasion. "He denied, saying, I know not, neither understand I what thou sayest." This complete disavowal of all knowledge of the Lord Jesus Christ came from the lips of one who had made such great protestations of loyalty. Then Peter was recognized by another servant-girl. She immediately pointed him out to others as a follower of Jesus, but a second time the fearful disciple disowned all knowledge of Christ.

Then others led by a relative of Malchus, whose ear Peter had cut off as he slashed about with his sword (John 18:26), accused him. They even called attention to his rough Galilean accent as evidence that he belonged to the band of those who were known to be disciples of Christ. "He began to curse and to swear, saying, I know not this man of whom ye speak." Terrified, Peter reverted to the language of his unconverted days and declared with oaths that he did not know the Lord Jesus Christ at all. To what depths may the believer fall if he gets out of fellowship with his Lord!

The crowing of a cock (the second time that early morning)

brought Peter to his senses and he remembered with grief the words of the Lord Jesus, who had forewarned him of this very failure.

The difference between apostasy and backsliding is illustrated clearly in the records concerning Judas and Simon Peter. Apostasy is a complete rejection of the truth and hence of Him who came to proclaim it and who is Himself the way, the truth, and the life. One may profess faith in Christ and give outward adherence to His teaching without ever being born again. In the hour of severe temptation such a one may apostatize, completely repudiating all he once professed to believe. For the apostate there is no promise of restoration. Backsliding, on the other hand, is a lowering of one's spiritual experience until in the hour of testing there is no strength to stand and so failure may come in to mar one's testimony. But the Lord says He is married to the backsliding one and He will bring about restoration eventually (Jeremiah 3:14). Peter was a backslider. Though he fell into grievous sin, he soon realized his wretched plight and returned in deep penitence to the Lord he had denied.

CHAPTER FIFTEEN

THE SUPREME SACRIFICE
PART TWO

Pilate's Court (Mark 15:1-15)

We come now to the great crisis that had been in the mind of our Lord from the beginning of His sojourn here on earth. This crisis had in fact brought Him from the glory that was His with the Father before all worlds began, into this world where sin defiled the fair creation.

Details given in the other Gospels are omitted in Mark's account. The scene moves rapidly from the council of the Jewish leaders to Pilate's judgment hall and then to the cross. There is no mention of the court of Herod, nor of other matters on which the Spirit of God led the other writers to elaborate.

Early in the morning the high priest summoned the Sanhedrin together and with their endorsement bound Jesus as though He were a dangerous criminal. As soon as Pilate was prepared to hold court they delivered Him up to be judged according to Roman law and executed as an insurrectionist. They knew that the trumped-up charge of blasphemy would mean nothing to the procurator who was acting as representative of the imperial government.

Crafty, self-seeking, and relentlessly cruel, Pilate was a scheming politician who regarded the rights of no man if to maintain them might prove an embarrassment to himself. He was thoroughly convinced of both the innocence of Jesus and the enmity behind the accusation brought by the leaders in Israel. But he quailed before the threat embodied in the words, "If thou let this man go, thou art not Caesar's friend" (John 19:12). Fearing that his political enemies might misrepresent him before the emperor, Pilate chose to sacrifice the Lord Jesus in order to retain the favor of Rome. (In Pilate's eyes Jesus was an unimportant Galilean artisan turned teacher.) Consequently his name has gone down in infamy throughout the centuries, his dishonor embodied in the words of the creed: "Christ ...suffered under Pontius Pilate."

The leaders accused Jesus of proclaiming Himself the rightful King of the Jews and gathering a group of malcontents with the intention of delivering Israel from the Roman yoke. Pilate put the question directly to the prisoner, "Art thou the King of the Jews?" Jesus replied, "Thou sayest it"—that is, "You have said that which is indeed the truth." For He surely was King of the Jews, though the time had not yet come to claim the throne of David. Vehemently the chief priests shouted out one accusation after another against Jesus, to which He made no reply.

Marveling at the calmness of the lowly man who stood so meekly before him, Pilate asked Him, "Answerest thou nothing?" Then he added, "Behold how many things they witness against thee." But Jesus, as the prophet Isaiah had foretold, opened not his mouth (Isaiah 53:7).

Pilate was perplexed. He saw through the priests and scribes' pretended concern for the honor of the empire. He realized that they were moved by a spirit of envy against this man who had captivated the imagination of so many. There can be no doubt that Pilate had heard much of the sayings and miracles of Jesus, for his agents were everywhere. He knew well why the leaders in Israel hated the Nazarene.

Pilate considered how he might release Jesus without angering these haughty ecclesiastics. He recalled that some time before, Rome had authorized him to release one political prisoner at the Passover season in order to placate the Jews, leaving the choice to them. He thought of an actual insurrectionist who was once followed by many, but who was now awaiting execution, and Pilate decided to offer the people the choice of this malefactor or Jesus.

The name *Barabbas* means "son of the father." Some ancient

manuscripts call him Jesus Barabbas. He was well-known as a leader in a revolt against the Roman rule over Palestine and had participated in an insurrection in which he had been guilty of murder. Evidently he was a hero in the eyes of the rabble, for they at once began to cry out, begging Pilate that he would follow the custom referred to above and give them their choice of a prisoner to be released.

Pilate agreed to this, but hoped it would free him from any further responsibility concerning Jesus. So he inquired, "Will ye that I release unto you the King of the Jews?" The title was used by him sardonically, as though he recognized in Jesus a rebel against Rome, for in his heart he knew the real reason back of their hatred for Jesus.

"The chief priests moved the people," who were easily swayed in such a scene of excitement, and stirred them to ask for Barabbas, which they did. The choice that was made that day between Jesus and Barabbas is also the choice that the nations have been making all down through the centuries. Thus Barabbas became, as it were, a figure of the antichrist.

"What will ye then that I shall do unto him whom ye call the King of the Jews?" Pilate vainly endeavored to forego all responsibility in the matter. He put the question of Jesus' fate to them in such a way as to make them feel that the final decision was their own.

"They cried out again, Crucify him." These base religious leaders demanded a cruel death for Him who had so often rebuked them for their hypocrisy.

The Roman judge knew Jesus had broken no law of the empire and therefore did not deserve to die. But Pilate was too much afraid of the Jews to take a positive stand against them. The rabble, stirred up by the priests, demanded the crucifixion of the One against whom no evil could be proved.

Pilate should have maintained the right of the innocent but he was more concerned about conciliating the Jews than protecting Christ. So he who had a little while before declared Him a just person (Matthew 27:24) sentenced Him to die by crucifixion. If Pilate had been a conscientious judge, he would have refused to countenance the unproved charges of Christ's adversaries and set Him free. But God overruled and used him as the instrument to fulfill the prophecy regarding the manner of Christ's death.

The Soldiers' Cruelty (Mark 15:16-24)

After Pilate's pusillanimous behavior in giving in to the chief priests and condemning Jesus, the Lord was led from the judgment hall to the outer court called the Praetorium. There the soldiers subjected the patient sufferer to a season of rude mockery and torture.

They had heard the charge that Jesus claimed to be a king; so with fiendish glee they pretended to acknowledge Him as such, clothing Him with a purple robe as a sign of apparent recognition of His royalty. They pressed on His sacred brow a crown made of the wild thorn bush so common to the countryside. Bowing before Him in mock humiliation they saluted Him: "Hail, King of the Jews!" To these rude soldiers this was all an absurd jest. In spite of all the barbarities they heaped on Jesus, they were not half as guilty as those of His own people who had demanded His crucifixion.

After satisfying their sadistic desire for pleasure the soldiers divested Jesus of the robe and put His own garments on Him. They proceeded to lead Him out to the place of crucifixion. A heavy cross was placed on His shoulders that He might bear it to Calvary, or Golgotha. Tradition says He fell beneath the weight of it, but there is no such statement in Scripture. We are told only that a Cyrenian named Simon, here designated as the father of Alexander and Rufus, was conscripted to bear the cross and thus relieve the condemned One. The early Christians said that this Cyrenian and his sons all became loyal followers of Jesus in later days. Some identify one of the sons with the Rufus mentioned in Romans 16:13.

"The place of a skull." Many believe that this refers to the skull-shaped hill outside Jerusalem, near the Damascus gate. This hill is known as Gordon's Calvary. Others understand the words to refer simply to the place of execution. *Golgotha, Calvary, the place of a skull*—what sacred memories cluster around these words! Before our Lord was crucified they meant nothing to anyone except that they designated a place outside the walls of Jerusalem where criminals—offenders against the laws of mighty Rome—were executed. But for more than nineteen centuries since the Son of man was lifted up, the name *Calvary*, or its equivalent in other tongues, has stirred the hearts of millions. That name has become the symbol of a love that was stronger than death, a love that the many waters of judgment could not quench.

The soldiers offered the Lord Jesus a drink, but He would not partake of the wine mixed with myrrh. This stupefying draught was prepared in order to assuage the suffering of those dying by crucifixion. He would not accept anything that might hinder His entering fully into all that the cross involved.

"They parted his garments, casting lots upon them." In this activity the soldiers were fulfilling unknowingly the prophecy of David, uttered over a thousand years before and recorded in Psalm 22:18. A criminal's garments were recognized as part of the perquisites of the soldiers officiating at a crucifixion.

From the moment when He came forth from the Father to the stable of Bethlehem, the cross was ever before our blessed Lord. He became man in order that He might be the propitiation for our sins (1 John 2:2). One of our hymn writers said it well:

> His path, uncheered by earthly smiles,
> Led only to the cross.

At Calvary the sin question was settled for eternity when He, the sinless One, was made sin—that is, became a sin offering—that "we might be made the righteousness of God in him" (2 Corinthians 5:21).

The Crucifixion (Mark 15:25-39)

Christ was crucified at "the third hour," counting according to Roman time from sunrise, which we call six o'clock.

"His accusation...THE KING OF THE JEWS." It was customary to fasten placards above the heads of those crucified to indicate the nature of their offense. Pilate ironically designated Jesus the King of the Jews, assigning Him the crime of rebellion against the Roman authority.

The two thieves who were crucified with Christ were actually guilty of crimes against the law of the land. Seven centuries before

Isaiah had written of Christ, "He was numbered with the transgressors" (Isaiah 53:12). Now his words were fulfilled literally. The Gospel of Mark records neither the conversation of the crucified men nor the confession of the one who cried to Jesus for deliverance (see Luke 23:39-43).

"They that passed by railed on him." With no pity for His grief and agony, the jeering mob distorted His words and flung them in His face. They taunted Him and called on Him to demonstrate His power by descending from the cross if He were indeed the anointed of God. They did not realize that it was their sins that held Him on that tree, not the nails that were driven through His hands and feet.

"He saved others; himself he cannot save." The chief priests uttered these words in mockery but they were declaring a tremendous fact. If He would save others He could not save Himself.

"Let Christ the King of Israel descend now from the cross, that we may see and believe." In cruel irony they addressed Him by the very titles that were His by right, but He did not respond. To descend from the cross would have meant the eternal doom of all our fallen race.

We note with awe and reverence that for six dreadful hours the Son of God hung on that cross of shame. These six hours are divided very definitely into two parts. From the third to the sixth hour—that is, from what we would call nine o'clock in the morning till noon—the sun was shining, and all could see what was transpiring. During those three hours Jesus Christ was suffering at the hands of man. For all their malignancy men have to be judged unless repentance lead them to turn for salvation to the One they crucified (Acts 2:23; Psalm 69:20-28). Yet it was not what men inflicted upon Him that put away sin (Hebrews 9:26).

From the sixth to the ninth hour darkness spread over all the scene. No human eye could pierce that gloom. It was then that Messiah's soul was made an offering for sin. As that supernatural darkness covered the scene, a terrible sense of horror must have struck the souls of the ribald multitude. It was in those three hours that the cup of judgment was pressed to the Savior's lips and drained to the dregs, that we might drink of the cup of salvation (Psalm 116:13).

"Eloi, Eloi, lama sabachthani?" The words are Aramaic and are found in Psalm 22:1—"My God, my God, why hast thou forsaken me?" Elizabeth Barrett Browning called these words "Immanuel's orphaned cry." They tell us, as nothing else could, of the awful abandonment of soul into which the Lord Jesus Christ went when He became the great sin bearer. It was then that God, the righteous Judge, dealt with Christ as the surety standing in the sinner's stead. Impenitent sinners will yet have to experience this abandonment.

"Behold, he calleth Elias." These were the words of one who did not understand the Aramaic and thought the cry "Eloi" was addressed to the prophet Elijah.

As the darkness passed away Jesus recalled one prophecy yet unfulfilled (Psalm 69:21) and He cried, "I thirst" (John 19:28-29). In answer to His cry a sponge filled with vinegar was pressed to His parched lips (Mark 15:36). The Lord Jesus Christ refused the cup of myrrh and wine, but drank of the vinegar. The first was calculated to bring about insensibility. He would not permit this. The other spoke of the sourness and bitterness of man's attitude toward Him. He accepted this without a murmur.

"Jesus cried with a loud voice." He did not die from exhaustion. He dismissed His spirit when all was accomplished (Matthew 27:50).

God's hand tore the temple veil in two, signifying that the way into the holiest had now been opened up (Hebrews 10:19-20). God need no longer dwell in the thick darkness (2 Chronicles 6:1). He could come out in the light, and man could go in to Him because of the cleansing blood of Christ (1 John 1:7).

"Truly this man was the Son of God." Convinced by what he saw and heard, the Roman centurion in charge of the crucifixion declared his personal faith in the supernaturalness of the holy sufferer who had just died on that cross.

The crucifixion of our Lord Jesus was far more than a martyrdom for truth; though it was that too (John 18:37). The cross was the display of God's hatred against sin and His infinite love for lost mankind. We should never think of Calvary as though it simply involved an innocent man dying for guilty men. It was God giving Himself in the person of His Son to bear the judgment that His righteous law declared to be the penalty of sin. There "the Offended died to set the offender free." Because of what Christ endured there, expiation has been made for iniquity and now God can "be just, and the justifier of him which believeth in Jesus" (Romans 3:26). God grant that our hearts may ever be tender and that our spirits may be deeply moved as we consider anew the Savior's death on Calvary.

The Burial (Mark 15:40-47)

There is something tenderly pathetic about the little company of faithful women to whom the Lord Jesus Christ was precious. Bewildered and perplexed as they must have been, they stood at some distance, beholding the One whom they had believed to be the Messiah of Israel, God's anointed King, dying on a cross of shame.

Mark mentioned two women by the name of Mary: Mary Magdalene, and Mary the mother of James and of Joses—that is, of James and Jude, two of the apostles. He did not mention Mary the mother of our Lord. We know, however, from John's account that she stood by the cross until her dying Son commended her to the care of the beloved apostle John.

Salome and some others had come from Galilee to be near Him and hear His gracious messages. What must have been the thoughts of their hearts when they beheld Him apparently powerless in the hand of His enemies! Did they remember what His apostles had forgotten: that He had promised He would rise again the third day? Apparently not, for we find afterward that His resurrection was as great a wonder to these women as it was to any of His other friends.

Isaiah wrote seven hundred years before the crucifixion that Jesus would be with the rich in His death (Isaiah 53:9). And so when our Lord had given up His life, Joseph of Arimathaea, a member of the high council of Israel, came boldly to Pilate and asked for the body of the crucified Savior. Joseph was a disciple in secret and waited for the kingdom of God, but now he came out into the open identifying himself with the rejected Christ.

Those who were put to death by crucifixion often lingered not only for many hours but even for days on their crosses before death brought relief from their sufferings. So Pilate could hardly believe that Jesus was already dead. He called the centurion who had been in charge of the execution and inquired of him whether Jesus was actually dead. When Pilate was assured that it was indeed true he commanded that the body should be entrusted to Joseph, who reverently and tenderly took the body down from the cross. In accordance with the Jewish burial customs he wrapped the precious form in the fine linen he had bought. He laid the body in his own new tomb, a sepulcher that was hewn out of a rock close by the place of crucifixion. After rolling a great stone across the entrance of the sepulcher, Joseph went his way.

Mary Magdalene and the other Mary stood at some distance looking on, observing where Jesus was laid. It was their thought to come back to the tomb as soon as the sabbath was passed and properly embalm the body that had been so hastily placed in the sepulcher. But this was not to be, for God was about to manifest His power and express His approval of the work of His beloved Son by raising Him in triumph from the tomb.

CHAPTER SIXTEEN
CHRIST SERVING STILL

The Resurrection (Mark 16:1-8)

The last sabbath of the law that God ever recognized had drawn to a close. During that old covenant rest day no one on earth knew whether redemption had been accomplished or not. The Jews observed the rest although their hands were red with the blood of the servant of Jehovah. They had insisted on His death, and in so doing had fulfilled their own Scriptures without realizing it. Now the first day of a new week and of a new dispensation had dawned.

Several godly women who were last at the cross were first at the tomb on that wondrous Easter morn. As the first streaks of light shone across the sky three women with broken hearts—Mary Magdalene, Mary the mother of James the less, and Salome—left their homes and wended their way toward the garden tomb in which the body of Jesus had been placed. They intended to anoint and embalm that precious body in the Jewish manner.

As the sun rose higher they came in sight of the tomb. Coming closer, the women wondered who would move the great stone blocking the entrance. This stone was probably like a large millstone fitted into a slot cut in the limestone on an incline so that it could be readily rolled down the groove to cover the door. But it would take considerable strength to roll it back and up again. None of the disciples were on hand to do this service. They mourned the death of Jesus and evidently thought there was nothing now that they could do to change things for the better.

But as the women came closer they were astonished to see that the stone was rolled back already and the entrance plainly revealed.

Their first thought, we know from other accounts, was that the tomb had been rifled by the enemies of Jesus and the body stolen and carried elsewhere.

On entering the sepulcher they beheld "a young man sitting on the right side, clothed in a long white garment." His presence filled the women with a strange alarm. Little did they understand at the moment that this young man had been present at the creation of the universe "when the morning stars sang together, and all the sons of God shouted for joy" (Job 38:7). The man possessed eternal youth, for he belonged not to earth but to Heaven. At once he reassured them and told them not to be afraid. He added, "Ye seek Jesus of Nazareth, which was crucified: he is risen; he is not here: behold the place where they laid him."

The dark night of death was not the end of the service of our blessed Lord. For Him the "path of life" led out of the tomb up to the glory where, at the Father's right hand, there are pleasures forevermore. His soul was not left in Hades—the unseen world—nor did His precious body see corruption in the sepulcher (Psalm 16). Isaiah had declared by the Spirit of prophecy, "When thou shalt make his soul an offering for sin, he shall see his seed, he shall prolong his days, and the pleasure of the Lord shall prosper in his hand" (Isaiah 53:10). So He "who was delivered for our offences...was raised again for our justification" (Romans 4:25). Because His death had met every claim of the justice of God against us, His resurrection was the divine declaration of our justification from all things.

With wondering eyes the women gazed on the empty crypt where only the graveclothes remained. The angel (for such he was) commanded them to go their way and tell the disciples and Peter that Jesus was going before them into Galilee to that meeting place of which He had told them before He was crucified. There He would manifest Himself to them. So the women hastened toward the city, but they were afraid to tell anyone what they had seen and heard.

There is something peculiarly touching about the two words "and Peter" (Mark 16:7). Peter must have spent the time of his Lord's entombment in grief and agony of soul as he pondered his denial. He would not feel worthy any longer to be called one of His disciples.

But the special message, "and Peter," would be the assurance that Jesus loved him still and counted him as one of His own.

Jesus Appears to Many (Mark 16:9-14)

"He appeared first to Mary Magdalene." One of the women evidently lingered in the garden and Jesus Himself appeared to her. There seems to be no Scriptural evidence that this Mary was ever a dissolute immoral woman, as so many have supposed. Down through the centuries *magdalene* has been synonymous with *harlot* because many have sought to identify Mary of Magdala with the "woman in the city" who came into the Pharisee's house and washed the feet of Jesus with her tears of repentance (Luke 7:37-39). But there seems to be no proof that the two are identical. What we are told in Mark 16 is that Jesus had cast seven demons out of Mary. Her love was great because her deliverance had been so great. Many an otherwise respectable woman has been demon-controlled at times. It is not necessary to suppose that demon possession implies unchastity.

Jesus revealed Himself to Mary in the garden in such a way that all her doubts were gone (John 20:11-18). She hastened to tell His disciples, who were mourning and weeping over the death of their Lord, that He was indeed risen from the dead. Though she confidently affirmed that she had seen and talked with Him, they did not believe that He who had died was alive again. Mark did not mention the visit of John and Peter to the tomb, and their corroboration of the story of Mary.

Mark told us in few words that which Luke described so fully—the meeting of Jesus with the two disciples on the road to Emmaus (see Luke 24:13-35). From the words "He appeared in another form" (Mark 16:12) some have drawn the erroneous conclusion that after resurrection Jesus no longer possessed the identical body in which He was crucified. Other Scriptures forbid such a thought. The Gospel of Luke tells us that the eyes of the two disciples were blinded to Jesus' true identity. He had not assumed a different body. As the two sat with Him at supper He revealed Himself to them. They returned to Jerusalem and told the eleven that they had seen Him; but again we read, "Neither believed they them." It was difficult to convince the apostles that Jesus had overcome death.

Jesus had foretold again and again His rising from the dead after three days; but His disciples were dull of hearing and failed to comprehend the meaning of His words. Therefore the resurrection was unexpected, and it took them some time to accept so marvelous a fact. Only the clearest demonstration of His resurrection convinced them of the truth.

The last appearance that Mark mentioned took place as the disciples were partaking of their evening meal. Whether Mark was referring to the same occasion as that mentioned in Luke 24:36-43 and John 20:19 we may not be able to decide. In all probability the appearance recorded in Mark 16:14 was either on the first evening following Jesus' resurrection when Thomas was absent, or another time when he was there. As some were still unbelieving, the Lord "upbraided them with their unbelief and hardness of heart." They had not accepted the testimony of the women and of Cleopas and his companion, who only confirmed what Jesus Himself had told them would take place. This rebuke seems to fit in with the occasion when Thomas was absent, for all doubt seems to have gone from the others when Thomas first saw the risen Lord. But it is important to keep their original unbelief in mind as we go on to consider what He told them afterward.

Christ's Final Command (Mark 16:15-20)

The great commission was not given at one time only, but on several occasions, and in each instance there are differences that are of deep interest. In Mark 16:15-18 Jesus set forth His program of world evangelization in no uncertain terms. "Preach the gospel to every creature." The disciples were to carry the good news of an accomplished redemption not only to Israel, to whom the message of the kingdom had been largely confined during the Lord's earthly ministry (Matthew 10:6), but "into all the world." Every barrier was to be thrown down so that the river of grace might flow out to all.

"He that believeth and is baptized shall be saved." Those who received the message in faith were to witness to it by being baptized, thus declaring themselves openly as His disciples. There was no saving virtue in the ordinance itself, but it was the expression of subjection to Christ. Those who refused to believe would be condemned. Note that He did not say, "He that is not baptized shall be condemned."

"These signs shall follow them that believe." These signs were what Paul calls "the signs of an apostle" (2 Corinthians 12:12). These miraculous powers were given to the authoritative messengers to accredit them as Christ's representatives (Acts 4:30-33; 5:12). But the signs were not displayed by any who did not believe, and even among the twelve "some doubted" (Matthew 28:17). It is a mistake to suppose that these powers were automatically passed on to those who believed the messengers. That is not the thought. Such gifts were granted to some who became witnesses publicly (1 Corinthians 12:7-11), but the bestowal of gifts was according to the sovereign will of God.

The Gospel of Mark does not tell us how much time elapsed between the giving of this commission and the ascension of Christ. Other records indicate that nearly forty days transpired. At the appointed time the man Christ Jesus was received up into glory (1 Timothy 3:16), where He now shares the Father's throne (Hebrews 1:3).

"They went forth...the Lord working with them." All that His servants accomplish for Him is actually done by Him as He works in and through them in the energy of His Holy Spirit. We are told that the disciples "preached every where." We know from the book of Acts that they were slow in doing this. It was some time before they could divest themselves of their Jewish prejudices in order to be free to go into all the world and make known the good news to the Gentiles. But as time went on they understood more fully the mind of the Lord and so went everywhere as He had commanded them.

The book of Acts and the history of missions attest to the authenticity of the post-resurrection appearances of Christ and the giving of the great commission. The work of world evangelization is in progress still, and will not be completed until all men everywhere have heard the message of the grace of God. Interest in missions is not an elective in God's university of grace. It is something in which every disciple is expected to major. We who are saved have been entrusted by our risen Lord with the glorious privilege of carrying the gospel to the whole world. It is for this very purpose we have been left in this world. As far as our own salvation is concerned, we were as secure as God could make us the first moment we trusted in Christ. We could have been taken home to Heaven immediately. But in the infinite wisdom of God we have been kept down here that we might be witnesses to His saving grace and that through us many more might be brought to share the blessings that are ours in Christ. Had the church been faithful to its commission, the body of Christ might long since have been completed and the Lord's return hastened, for it is due to His concern for the salvation of men that He seems to delay (2 Peter 3:9).

After Mark recorded the great commission, he did not go on to describe the ascension, but he closed his account with the risen Lord as the servant still working with His followers as they go forth in obedience to His Word.

A HARMONY OF THE GOSPELS

	Matthew	Mark	Luke	John
Genealogies of Jesus	1:1-17		3:23-38	
The Coming Forerunner			1:5-25	
Annunciation to Mary			1:26-38	
The Magnificat			1:46-56	
Birth of John the Baptist			1:57-80	
Birth of Jesus	1:18-25		2:1-7	
The Message of the Angels			2:8-20	
The Presentation in the Temple			2:21-38	
Visit of the Magi	2:1-12			
Flight into Egypt	2:13-15			
Vengeance of Herod	2.16-23			
The Childhood of Jesus			2:39-52	
John the Baptist's Ministry	3:1-12	1:2-8	3:1-22	1:6-14
John Baptizes Jesus	3:13-17	1:9-11	3:21-22	
Jesus Is Tempted	4:1-11	1:12-13	4:1-13	
The Testimony of John the Baptist				1:15-36
Initial Calling of Disciples				1:35-51
Jesus' First Miracle				2:1-11
First Cleansing of the Temple				2:12-25

	Matthew	Mark	Luke	John
Talk with Nicodemus				3:1-21
John the Baptist's Final Testimony				3:22-36
Woman at the Well				4:1-26
The Conversion of the Samaritans				4:27-42
Jesus Begins Ministry in Galilee	4:12-17			
Healing of Nobleman's Son				4:46-54
Jesus Is Rejected at Nazareth			4:14-30	
Jesus Calls His First Disciples	4:18-25	1:14-20	5:1-11	
Jesus Casts Out Demons		1:21-28	4:31-37	
Jesus Heals Peter's Mother-in-law	8:14-17	1:29-34	4:38-41	
Jesus Cleanses a Leper	8:1-4	1:35-45	5:12-15	
Jesus Heals a Paralytic	9:1-8	2:1-12	5:16-26	
Calling of Matthew	9:9-13	2:13-17	5:27-32	
Healing and Teaching at Pool of Bethesda				5:1-47
Jesus Defends His Disciples	9:14-17	2:18-22	5:33-39	
Defining Sabbath Day Observance	12:1-8	2:23-28	6:1-11	
Jesus Heals on the Sabbath	12:9-21	3:1-6	6:6-11	
Multitudes Healed	12:15-21	3:7-12		
Jesus Ordains the Twelve		3:13-19	6:12-16	
Sermon on the Mount	5:1–7:29		6:17-49	
Jesus Heals the Centurion's Servant	8:5-13		7:1-10	

	Matthew	Mark	Luke	John
Jesus Raises the Widow's Son			7:11-18	
Jesus Testifies to the Greatness of John the Baptist	11:1-19		7:19-35	
Jesus Proclaims Misery on Unrepentant Cities	11:20-24		10:13-15	
Jesus Offers Rest for the Weary	11:25-30			
Jesus Teaches of Forgiveness			7:36-50	
Jesus Confirms His Authority	12:22-30	3:22-27	11:14-28	
The Unpardonable Sin	12:31-37	3:28-30	12:10	
Jesus Condemns Jews' Unbelief	12:38-45		11:29-54	
Jesus Introduces a New Family	12:46-50	3:31-35	8:19-21	
Parables of the Kingdom	13:1-53	4:1-34	8:1-15; 13:18-21	
Power over Creation	8:23-27	4:35-41	8:22-25	
Gadarene Demoniac Healed	8:28-34	5:1-20	8:26-39	
Jairus's Daughter Raised	9:18-19, 23-26	5:21-24, 35-43	8:40-42, 49-56	
Woman with Issue of Blood Healed	9:20-22	5:25-34	8:43-48	
Healing of Blind and Mute	9:27-34			
The Prophet Without Honor	13:54-58	6:1-6		
Jesus Sends Out His Couriers	9:35–10:15	6:7-13	9:1-11	
Warning of Coming Persecution	10:16-23			

	Matthew	Mark	Luke	John
Promise of Care and Comfort	10:24-33			
Warning of Conflict	10:34-39			
Reward for Those who Accept His Couriers	10:40-42			
John the Baptist Murdered	14:1-14	6:14-29	9:7-9	
Five Thousand Fed	14:15-21	6:33-46	9:11-17	6:1-15
Jesus Walks on Water	14:22-36	6:47-52		6:16-21
The Food that Endures				6:22-71
Jesus Condemns Pharisaic Tradition	15:1-20	7:1-23		
Jesus Rewards the Faith of a Gentile Woman	15:21-28	7:24-30		
Jesus Opens Ears of Deaf		7:31-37		
Four Thousand Fed	15:29-39	8:1-9		
Pharisees Demand a Sign	16:1-4	8:10-13		
Jesus Warns His Disciples	16:5-12	8:14-21	12:1-21	
A Blind Man Healed		8:22-26		
Peter's Confession	16:13-20	8:27-30	9:18-21	
Christ Foretells His Death and Resurrection	16:21-26	8:31-37	9:22-25	
Christ Tells of the Coming of His Kingdom	16:27-28	8:38–9:1	9:26-27	
The Transfiguration	17:1-8	9:2-8	9:28-36	
Explanation of the Coming of Elijah	17:9-13	9:9-13		
Demon-Possessed Boy Healed	17:14-21	9:14-29	9:37-43	
Christ Again Foretells His Death and Resurrection	17:22-23	9:30-32	9:44-45	

	Matthew	Mark	Luke	John
Payment of Temple Tax	17:24-27			
Greatest in the Kingdom	18:1-14	9:33-50	9:46-50	
Lessons in Forgiveness	18:15-35		17:3-4	
Attitudes of World toward Christ				7:1-53
Rebuking Intolerance			9:51-56	
Cost of Discipleship	8:19-22		9:57-62	
Woman Taken in Adultery				8:1-11
The Light of the World				8:12-20
Salvation After Death?				8:21-32
Children of the Devil				8:33-47
The Pre-existent Christ				8:48-59
Man Born Blind Healed				9:1-41
The Good Shepherd				10:1-16
The Mission of the Seventy			10:1-20	
The Mystery of the Incarnation			10:21-24	
Parable of the Good Samaritan			10:25-37	
Service and Fellowship			10:38-42	
Teaching on Prayer			11:1-13	
Warning of Danger of Covetousness			12:13-21	
Living Without Anxiety			12:22-34	
Waiting for the Lord's Return			12:35-48	
The Offense of the Cross			12:49-59	
A Call to Repentance			13:1-9	

	Matthew	Mark	Luke	John
Crippled Woman Healed on the Sabbath			13:10-17	
Security of Christ's Sheep				10:17-30
Jesus's Works Testify to His Deity				10:31-42
A Great Crisis			13:22-35	
Jesus Heals Again on the Sabbath			14:1-6	
Parable of the Ambitious Guest			14:7-14	
Parable of the Great Supper			14:15-24	
Counting the Cost			14:25-35	
Lost Ones Found			15:1-32	
Parable of the Unjust Steward			16:1-17	
Teaching on Divorce	19:1-12	10:1-12	16:18	
The Rich Man and Lazarus			16:19-31	
Subjection to Christ			17:1-10	
Ten Lepers Cleansed			17:11-19	
Teaching on Christ's Second Advent			17:20-37	
Persistence in Prayer			18:1-8	
Right Attitude in Prayer			18:9-14	
Raising of Lazarus				11:1-46
One Man to Die				11:47-54
Christ Blesses Children	19:13-15	10:13-16	18:15-17	
Rich Young Ruler	19:16-30	10:17-31	18:18-30	
Parable of the Laborers	20:1-16			

	Matthew	Mark	Luke	John
Third Prediction by Christ of His Death	20:17-19	10:32-34	18:31-34	
Worldly Ambition	20:20-28	10:35-45		
Healing the Blind	20:29-34	10:46-52	18:35-43	
Jesus Meets Zacchaeus			19:1-10	
Parable of the Pounds			19:11-27	
The Triumphal Entry	21:1-11	11:1-11	19:28-44	12:12-19
Second Cleansing of Temple	21:12-16	11:12-19	19:45-48	
Jesus Predicts His Death				12:20-36
Christ Still Rejected				12:37-43
Christ: Not Judge But Savior				12:44-50
Jesus Curses the Fig Tree	21:17-22	11:12-14, 19-26		
Jesus Affirms His Authority	21:23-27	11:27-33	20:1-8	
Parable of the Two Sons	21:28-32			
Parable of the Vineyard	21:33-46	12:1-12	20:9-20	
Parable of the Wedding Feast	22:1-14			
Lesson on Paying Taxes	22:15-22	12:13-17	20:21-26	
Lesson on the Resurrection	22:23-33	12:18-27	20:27-40	
Lesson on the Great Commandment	22:34-40	12:28-34		
Lesson on Jesus' Identity	22:41-46	12:35-37	20:41-44	
Warning against Seeking Earthly Glory	23:1-12	12:38-40		
Woes on Religious Leaders	23:13-39		20:45-47	
Lesson on Giving		12:41-44	21:1-4	

	Matthew	Mark	Luke	John
Characteristics of Present Age	24:1-8	13:1-8	21:5-11	
Signs of Last Days	24:9-14	13:9-13	21:12-19	
Great Tribulation	24:15-28	13:14-23	21:20-24	
Coming of the Son	24:29-31	13:24-27	21:25-28	
The Sign of Christ's Coming	24:32-41	13:28-31	21:29-33	
Our Duty to Watch	24:42-51	13:32-37	21:34-38	
Parable of Ten Virgins	25:1-13			
Parable of Talents	25:14-30			
Sheep and Goats	25:31-46			
Mary's Devotion	26:1-13	14:1-9		12:1-11
Jesus Washes Disciples' Feet				13:1-17
The Last Passover	26:14-25	14:10-21	22:1-14	
Jesus Reveals the Betrayer	26:21-25	14:18-21	22:21-23	13:18-30
The Lord's Supper	26:26-30	14:22-25	22:15-20	
Jesus' Warning	26:31-35	14:27-31	22:24-38	13:31-38
Jesus Comforts His Disciples				14:1-31
Discourse on the Road to Gethsemane				15:1-27
The Work of the Holy Spirit				16:1-33
Jesus Prays for His Followers				17:1-26
Agony in the Garden	26:36-46	14:32-42	22:39-46	
Jesus' Arrest	26:47-56	14:43-50	22:47-53	18:1-11

	Matthew	Mark	Luke	John
Jesus before the Priests	26:57-68	14:53-65	22:63-71	18:12-14, 19-24
Peter's Denial	26:69-75	14:66-72	22:54-62	18:15-18, 25-27
Judas's Remorse	27:1-10			
Pilate's Court	27:11-18	15:1-10	23:1-5, 13-19	18:28-40
Herod's Court			23:6-12	
Pilate's Weakness	27:19-26	15:11-15	23:20-25	19:1-16
The Soldiers' Cruelty	27:27-32	15:16-21		19:1-3
The Crucifixion	27:33-44	15:22-32	23:26-43	19:17-27
Jesus' Death	27:45-56	15:33-41	23:44-49	19:28-37
Jesus' Burial	27:57-66	15:42-47	23:50-56	19:38-42
The Resurrection	28:1-10	16:1-8	24:1-12	
Peter and John at the Empty Tomb				20:1-10
Jesus Appears to Mary		16:9-11		20:11-18
The Road to Emmaus		16:12-13	24:13-35	
The Guard's Report	28:11-15			
Jesus with His Disciples				20:19-31
Miraculous Catch of Fish				21:1-14
Peter Reinstated				21:15-25
Christ's Final Command	28:16-20	16:15-20	24:36-49	
The Ascension		16:19	24:50-53	

AUTHOR BIOGRAPHY

HENRY ALLAN IRONSIDE, one of this century's greatest preachers, was born in Toronto, Canada, on October 14, 1876. He lived his life by faith; his needs at crucial moments were met in the most remarkable ways.

Though his classes stopped with grammar school, his fondness for reading and an incredibly retentive memory put learning to use. His scholarship was well recognized in academic circles with Wheaton College awarding an honorary Litt. D. in 1930 and Bob Jones University an honorary D.D. in 1942. Dr. Ironside was also appointed to the boards of numerous Bible institutes, seminaries, and Christian organizations.

"HAI" lived to preach and he did so widely throughout the United States and abroad. E. Schuyler English, in his biography of Ironside, revealed that during 1948, the year HAI was 72, and in spite of failing eyesight, he "gave 569 addresses, besides participating in many other ways." In his eighteen years at Chicago's Moody Memorial Church, his only pastorate, every Sunday but two had at least one profession of faith in Christ.

H. A. Ironside went to be with the Lord on January 15, 1951. Throughout his ministry, he authored expositions on 51 books of the Bible and through the great clarity of his messages led hundreds of thousands, worldwide, to a knowledge of God's Word. His words are as fresh and meaningful today as when first preached.

The official biography of Dr. Ironside, *H. A. Ironside: Ordained of the Lord*, is available from the publisher.

THE WRITTEN MINISTRY OF H. A. IRONSIDE

Expositions

Joshua	Acts
Ezra	Romans
Nehemiah	1 & 2 Corinthians
Esther	Galatians
Psalms (1-41 only)	Ephesians
Proverbs	Philippians
Song of Solomon	Colossians
Isaiah	1 & 2 Thessalonians
Jeremiah	1 & 2 Timothy
Lamentations	Titus
Ezekiel	Philemon
Daniel	Hebrews
The Minor Prophets	James
Matthew	1 & 2 Peter
Mark	1,2, & 3 John
Luke	Jude
John	Revelation

Doctrinal Works

Baptism	Letters to a Roman Catholic
Death and Afterward	Priest
Eternal Security of the Believer	The Levitical Offerings
Holiness: The False and	Not Wrath But Rapture
the True	Wrongly Dividing the Word
The Holy Trinity	of Truth

Historical Works

The Four Hundred Silent Years
A Historical Sketch of the Brethren Movement

Other works by the author are brought back into print from time to time. All of this material is available from your local Christian bookstore or from the publisher.

LOIZEAUX

A Heritage of Ministry . . .

Paul and Timothy Loizeaux began their printing and publishing activities in the farming community of Vinton, Iowa, in 1876. Their tools were rudimentary: a hand press, several fonts of loose type, ink, and a small supply of paper. There was certainly no dream of a thriving commercial enterprise. It was merely the means of supplying the literature needs for their own ministries, with the hope that the Lord would grant a wider circulation. It wasn't a business; it was a ministry.

Our Foundation Is the Word of God

We stand without embarrassment on the great fundamentals of the faith: the inspiration and authority of Scripture, the deity and spotless humanity of our Lord Jesus Christ, His atoning sacrifice and resurrection, the indwelling of the Holy Spirit, the unity of the church, the second coming of the Lord, and the eternal destinies of the saved and lost.

Our Mission Is to Help People Understand God's Word

We are not in the entertainment business. We only publish books we believe will be of genuine help to God's people, both through the faithful exposition of Scripture and practical application of its principles to contemporary need.

Faithfulness to the Word and consistency in what we publish have been hallmarks of Loizeaux through four generations. And that means when you see the name Loizeaux on the outside, you can trust what is on the inside. That is our promise to the Lord...and to you.

If Paul and Timothy were to visit us today they would still recognize the work they began in 1876. Because some very important things haven't changed at all...this is still a ministry.